What People Are Saying About Tim Elmore...

"No one teaches leadership better than Tim Elmore."

John Maxwell
bestselling author of more than 60 books

"Tim Elmore is a great communicator. His material is relevant and helpful. I enjoyed his leadership teaching so much, I asked him to teach our entire staff."

Andy Stanley
founder and senior pastor,
North Point Community Church

"In our desire to be engaged parents, we sometimes do our kids more harm than good. We want to put them in a safe box, tell them not to leave it, and believe that all will be well. Tim's book inspires us to prepare our children for their adult lives, not our safe box! If we want them to thrive, we've got to equip them, and this book shows us how."

Jeremy Affeldt
pitcher, San Francisco Giants

"Our best intentions as parents can often lead to a series of unintended consequences that could dangerously derail the emotional development of our children. Once again, Dr. Tim Elmore combines research-based wisdom and practical application to keep us on track as we strive to nurture, love, and lead our children well. Buy this book. It's destined to become the well-worn manual of every mom and dad."

Tami Heim
former president of Borders Books
CEO, Christian Leadership Alliance

"As an educator and a student affairs practitioner with a background in mental health (and five chi_____) I highly endorse this important perspective on parenting in to_____s more complex than ever before. _____enefit from this commonsense a_____aching, supporting, and challengi_____learn, and to become the best people they can be."

Julie Talz Cox
director of residential life, Purdue University

"The challenges of life don't get easier as our kids grow older. In *12 Huge Mistakes Parents Can Avoid*, Dr. Tim Elmore reminds us that leading well as parents is critical if we expect our children to meet these challenges in every phase of their lives. We must be intentional, now more than ever. This book shows us how to not merely care for our kids, but to help them care for themselves."

Dayton Moore
general manager, Kansas City Royals

"When I first became a mom, I didn't really know what I didn't know. Like most parents, I learned valuable lessons from my mistakes. I wish I would have had Tim's guidance to help me back then. His researched and thoughtful approach makes this book a valuable resource for parents and other adults involved in the lives of children. The problem isn't that we neglect our children, but that we fail to prepare for each new life stage. Once again, Tim Elmore lays out a diagnosis and a prescription for what caring adults can do to help children mature."

Jo Kirchner
president and CEO, Primrose Schools

"As someone who teaches, advises, and researches college students, I found that *12 Huge Mistakes Parents Can Avoid* provides a relevant, practical framework for recognizing students' needs, understanding my role in their development, and acknowledging the way I can unknowingly hinder their progress. I recommend this book to any educator, especially those who work with students in transition. The 12 research-based mistakes are actually guideposts, offering us a lens to see the potential of who and what kids can be. Tim's voice is one of a mentor and a coach— asking powerful questions and sharing practical advice to bring out the best in us so we can bring out the best in our students."

Kerry Priest
assistant professor, Kansas State University School of Leadership Studies

12 HUGE MISTAKES PARENTS CAN AVOID

TIM ELMORE

HARVEST HOUSE PUBLISHERS
EUGENE, OREGON

Cover by Dugan Design Group, Bloomington, Minnesota

Cover photo © PhotoInc / E+ / Getty Images

Published in association with the literary agency of Wolgemuth & Associates, Inc.

This book contains stories in which peoples' names and some details of their circumstances have been changed to protect their identities.

12 HUGE MISTAKES PARENTS CAN AVOID
Copyright © 2014 by Tim Elmore
Published by Harvest House Publishers
Eugene, Oregon 97402
www.harvesthousepublishers.com

Library of Congress Cataloging-in-Publication Data
    Elmore, Tim.
    12 huge mistakes parents can avoid / Dr. Tim Elmore.
        pages cm
    ISBN 978-0-7369-5843-1 (pbk.)
    ISBN 978-0-7369-5844-8 (eBook)
    1. Parenting. 2. Parent and child. 3. Pampered child syndrome. I. Title II. Title: Twelve huge mistakes parents can avoid.
    HQ769.E56458 2014
    649'.1—dc23

                                                                2013044246

Printed in the United States of America

                15 16 17 18 19 20 21 22 / VP-JH / 10 9 8 7 6 5 4

Contents

Introduction

Allow me to introduce myself so that you won't misinterpret my words.

This book arises from my deep compassion for children and the adults who care for them. I lead a nonprofit organization called Growing Leaders, and we are in front of about 50,000 students, faculty, and parents each year. I love each and every one I meet. In addition, I am a father of two kids, Jonathan and Bethany, whom I love very, very much.

I love the moms and dads I meet every year. Many of these parents are heroes—especially the single parents who have to be both the good cop and the bad cop at home with their children.

We are about to discuss some of the most common mistakes we parents make today as we raise our kids. What I'll say may come across harshly, as if I lack compassion. Please know that I say what I do because I care. Today's mistakes are a bit different from the most common mistakes moms and dads may have made 50 years ago. We are pressured to form certain habits that our culture defines as good parenting habits but that are not good at all. Call it parental peer pressure. It pushes us to do things for our kids that actually hinder them from becoming healthy adults.

Let me illustrate.

Bullying has become a big issue on K-12 school campuses. In fact, some parents are obsessed with it. In the fall of 2013, the topic surfaced when a high school football team beat another team 91–0. It was quite a blowout.

The parent of a player on the losing team, Western Hills High School, accused the winning team, Aledo High School, of being bullies.

She filed a bullying complaint on the school's website, arguing that Aledo coaches should have eased up at some point. The Aledo coaches said they did—they benched their starters right after halftime, they stopped passing the ball, and they allowed the clock to run. The score could have easily been 150–0.

The story got mixed reviews. Some agreed with the parent, saying folks should be nicer to each other, especially when one team has far more talent than another. Others suggested these two teams simply shouldn't be playing each other, as Aledo High School has graduates heading to NCAA Division-1 universities. Yet others argued that calling a football game "bullying" is inappropriate given the real problems our country faces with school bullying.

Here's the challenge as I see it.

The truth is, we must find a way to cultivate empathy among students in a world where portable devices with screens have led to increased bullying, cyber-bullying, and diminishing emotional intelligence. As technology goes up, empathy goes down. I have spoken at countless schools about this issue and suggested that we must help kids see the big picture, envision the future, and act like leaders.

But take a moment and think about this parent's complaint.

To intervene and accuse coaches of bullying because of a game score is like scolding a teacher for giving an F on a paper or telling the teacher not to critique a student's assignment. When our kids are younger than 12, it is helpful to tell them exactly how to behave and perhaps even what to think. As they grow up, our control must decrease, and their coping skills must increase. By the time they're teens, this kind of intervention can be unhealthy. Here's why.

Healthy teens don't want adults to intervene in their relationships with peers. It's embarrassing. Some males have even compared it to shaving the mane off of a lion…the teen guys feel humiliated and weak. The parents may feel they've done the adolescent a favor, but in reality, they've done quite the opposite.

And as others have noted, a football score is nothing like a genuine bullying incident. Real bullying harms others. Losing a football game by a large score happens every week of the fall in America. It's part of life. To safeguard teens from this kind of thing actually hinders the development of their coping skills as they mature.

I lost plenty of games as an athlete growing up. In fact, in one Little League baseball season, our team lost every single game by large margins. I loved the way our manager never tried to sugarcoat the losses, but instead discussed with us what we'd learned and how we could improve. This prepared me for the adult world I was growing into.

No one would have dreamed of calling our blowout losses bullying. It would have been an insult to real bullying incidents, which occurred during the 1970s just as they do now. The difference between then and now is this: The adults in my childhood (including parents, teachers, coaches, and youth workers) helped us navigate these experiences rather than removing them from our lives. They knew that *hurt* does not equal *harm*. I think many adults are quite confused about this today.

Here's the bottom line. I believe we need to face some new issues as parents. We must define what kids need from us to mature in a healthy way. We must figure out what hinders their growth and what equips them to be great adults. We must become both nurturers *and* trainers, knowing that we are not raising children, but future adults. I offer this book as a reference guide as you face your toughest challenges and attempt to get kids ready for life as they leave your home or school. Here's to correcting our mistakes along the way—for their sake.

Dr. Tim Elmore
2014

The Overfunctioning Parent Quiz

Before you begin reading the book, respond to the questions below to assess your parenting style and preferences. Then add up your score to consider the potential mistakes that may hinder your child from growing into a healthy adult. Circle your most honest and accurate answers.

1. When my kids begin failing at a task, I try to help them out and prevent the failure.

1	2	3	4	5	6	7	8	9	10
Never		Seldom		Sometimes		Often		Always	

2. Regarding my children's future, I nudge them in a direction I wish I'd gone myself.

1	2	3	4	5	6	7	8	9	10
Never		Seldom		Sometimes		Often		Always	

3. My primary goal is my children's happiness, and that's what I hope they pursue.

1	2	3	4	5	6	7	8	9	10
Never		Seldom		Sometimes		Often		Always	

4. I'm so busy, I frequently relax on enforcing our house rules.

1	2	3	4	5	6	7	8	9	10
Never		Seldom		Sometimes		Often		Always	

5. When my children mess up, I come to their aid and fix the problem for them.

1	2	3	4	5	6	7	8	9	10
Never		Seldom		Sometimes		Often		Always	

6. I want my kids to have strong self-esteem, so I go overboard with praise for them.

1	2	3	4	5	6	7	8	9	10
Never		Seldom		Sometimes		Often		Always	

7. I find that I am unable to build a strong sense of ambition in my children.

1	2	3	4	5	6	7	8	9	10
Never		Seldom		Sometimes		Often		Always	

8. When my kids are struggling, I jump in and do it for them to relieve the stress.

1	2	3	4	5	6	7	8	9	10
Never		Seldom		Sometimes		Often		Always	

9. I buy things for my children that they want and can't seem to wait for.

1	2	3	4	5	6	7	8	9	10
Never		Seldom		Sometimes			Often		Always

10. I affirm my kids by telling them they are smart or beautiful or gifted.

1	2	3	4	5	6	7	8	9	10
Never		Seldom		Sometimes			Often		Always

11. I hurt so much when my kid experiences pain or setbacks, I try to prevent them.

1	2	3	4	5	6	7	8	9	10
Never		Seldom		Sometimes			Often		Always

12. When parenting my kids, I focus mainly on the issues and problems at hand today.

1	2	3	4	5	6	7	8	9	10
Never		Seldom		Sometimes			Often		Always

Total Your Score

Note were your highest numbers are. Those are generally the issues you'll want to focus on going forward. Each question corresponds with the list of mistakes in this book. Where you scored highest, pay special attention to the ideas on that chapter.

"I Get an A, You Get a D"

According to a recent nationwide survey, American parents gave themselves a grade of an A or a B on their parenting skills, but they gave all other parents a D.

What an interesting portrait of American adults in the twenty-first century—on so many levels.

As caring adults, we consistently believe we're sacrificing our blood, sweat, and tears for our children, and few realize the price we pay to parent, teach, or coach these kids. We work hard. At the same time, we look at our neighbor's kids or the students with whom our children attend school, and we are stunned that someone can't get them to behave better. Ahh…kids these days!

The fact is, it's difficult to be objective. When we evaluate our own leadership, we're acutely aware of the obstacles and hardships we've encountered just to make it through the day. We see how stressed-out our kids are, so we excuse their poor attitude or lack of discipline. We second-guess our decisions, not wanting to be too harsh or too wimpy as parents or teachers. We certainly don't want our kids to be seeing a therapist when they turn 30 because we didn't give them enough tender loving care. But later, we wonder if we've been too soft; we question whether these kids are ready for the real world when they graduate from high school.

When asked to consider the kind of example they set for their kids, parents got more honest. According to survey results from T. Rowe Price, nearly a third of parents were willing to admit they were not good role models at home.[1] Perhaps this kind of self-awareness is healthy. Maybe parents should get a report card. Think about it. We grade students every year in school. Why not ask adults to submit a grade for themselves on important priorities, such as managing money, attitudes, behavior, quality time spent with family, and the like? Interestingly, states are now passing legislation that will allow parents to do just that—to evaluate their involvement in their kids' lives at school. Utah, Louisiana, and Tennessee are among the first to do this.

Better still, why not allow the kids to grade the adults? After all, that's what we do to them. Author Ellen Galinsky reports what they think in her book *Ask the Children*. In her surveys, she has children separately grade their moms and dads in 12 areas. Then, she asks the parents the same questions. Can you guess the outcomes? Consistently, parents give themselves a higher grade than their children give them.[2]

Consider the question yourself. How are you doing? What grade would your kids give you right now as a parent? As a teacher? As an employer? As a coach? Even more importantly, what grade would they give you 20 years from now as they evaluated how well you prepared them for adulthood?

If we're doing so well, why aren't our kids more ready for the world that awaits them once they leave home? We cannot simply blame the economy or the government. A full one-third of our males between the ages of 22 and 34 still live at home with their parents.[3] In 2011, 80 percent of students reported they planned to move back home when they finished college.[4] Unfortunately, each level of school appears to merely prepare kids for more school, not for the real world. In 2000, more than 90 percent of teens planned on attending college. In 2012, nearly a third didn't even graduate from high school. Of those who went to college, most didn't finish.

After surveying corporations, one article reported that 50 percent of the jobs available to recent graduates went unfilled because the young people didn't possess the basic communication and leadership skills necessary for the positions. In other words, the jobs were ready, but the kids weren't. According to a sobering report from Condoleezza Rice and Joel Klein, the state of our young people has become an issue of national security. The Department of Defense estimates that 75 percent of young Americans are not even eligible to serve in the military because they didn't graduate from high school, are obese, or have criminal records.[5]

Somewhere along the way, we failed to get them ready.

A Generation of Firsts

Stop and reflect. In the same way the parents of the Baby Boomers were the first generation to raise their kids with the one-eyed babysitter—the TV—we are the first generation of parents to raise our kids with the Internet. They have a portable device in their hands 24/7. Culture seeps in, and we can do little about it. Consider a few of the firsts this generation has experienced.

They don't need adults to get information.

Consider how this difference changes the role of an adult. Because information is everywhere, we are no longer brokers of data. They don't need us for *information*, but for *interpretation*. We must help them make sense of all they know. Our job isn't to enable them to *access* data but to *process* data and form good decisions.

They can broadcast any thought or emotion to those who follow them.

You see this every week. Thanks to Twitter, Facebook, and Instagram, your kids can send messages to huge populations who matter. These applications are the new PR tools for your youth department or your school. Some posts actually get famous...for better or worse. Most kids who use these tools have not been equipped to harness their power.

They have external stimuli at their fingertips 24/7.

Because portable devices are in these kids' hands, they receive outside stimulation anytime they're bored. Consequently, many don't think well on their own. This outside entertainment may reduce their internal motivation. They've never had to motivate themselves. They depend on a screen to push them. We must equip them to find motivation from within.

They are socially connected at all times, but often in isolation.

This is the most connected generation in history—but perhaps the one that has experienced the least community. Kids are rarely disconnected, but still they are lonely, and they often connect virtually, in isolation, on a screen. As a result, their empathy, soft skills, and emotional intelligence remain undeveloped. They'll need those skills for life, but they've not been prepared.

They will learn more from a portable device than from a classroom.

This one is a game changer. The portable device they hold in their hand is now their compass. It guides them more than their teachers do. They'll consume more data on this device than through any other means. The data may be inaccurate or damaging, but it's available, and they are digesting it. They need us to help them navigate the flow of data and use this tool effectively.

They use a phone instead of a wristwatch, camera, wall calendar, alarm clock, or board game.

Students no longer manage their lives the way we did growing up. Their phone tells time, provides entertainment, takes pictures, gives directions, connects with friends, and broadcasts messages. Designed to make life simpler, this nonstop information center has made this the most stressed-out generation to date.

I began working with students in 1979. More than ever before, I see adults who are unsure how to lead, teach, parent, coach, pastor, and employ this generation of kids. Theories are everywhere, and the research on this paradoxical generation seems to contradict itself. Questions loom within us that our parents never faced.

- Should we limit kids' cell phone use?
- Should we use portable devices in the classroom? Is that good or bad?
- Do we become friends with our kids (or students) on Facebook?

- How much is too much time playing video games?
- Should we make our children play outside?
- What online safety measures should we take?
- How do we guard and guide their time on the Internet?
- How much freedom should we give our children with their friends?
- Do those friends need a background check?

These questions are but the tip of the iceberg. Consequently, we vacillate back and forth in our leadership of young people. We meddle, we lecture, we react and overreact, we poke around their Facebook profile, we review their recent cell phone calls and texts, hoping to find out what they need from us. Psychologists who once called us helicopter parents because we hover over our children now call us Apache helicopters. Sometimes, we actually do too much. In our attempts to help, we hinder.

Allow me to give you an analogy.

What's the Problem with Poking Around?

President James Garfield walked into the Baltimore and Potomac Railroad station in Washington, DC, on the humid morning of July 2, 1881, having no idea what awaited him. Lurking in the shadows that morning was Charles Guiteau, a crazy man with a pistol in his pocket. As soon as he saw Garfield, Guiteau stepped forward and fired two shots, one grazing the shoulder of the president, the other lodging just behind his pancreas. When the second bullet hit, the president fell to the ground.

Months later, Guiteau went on trial for the assassination of President Garfield and was found guilty. This, however, is not the saddest part of the story. Garfield actually died a pitiful and unnecessary death 11 weeks after the shooting.

During those 11 weeks, the self-appointed chief physician, Dr. D. Willard Bliss, stubbornly worked on Garfield, probing through his body to find the stray bullet. But alas, he could not. He had a team of other doctors working alongside him, but over time, he refused to let them even take Garfield's temperature or nurse his wound. Dr. Bliss was sure he was giving the president the finest of care. During the 80 days between the president's shooting and his death, Alexander Graham Bell visited with a metal detector he'd created to find the bullet. Dr. Bliss insisted he only search the right side of Garfield's body because he was convinced that was where the bullet lodged. Bell could not locate it.

Additionally, Joseph Lister offered some helpful guidance by suggesting the doctors wash their hands and utensils before using them to poke around inside the president's body. Lister had developed a theory on germs and infections arising from surgery performed without sanitizing everything. Sadly, Lister was scorned and even laughed at by physicians. They couldn't imagine tiny, invisible factors, such as germs, causing infections. Ridiculous.

In the end, James Garfield didn't die from the gunshot wounds. He could have recovered from them. It was Dr. Bliss's care of James Garfield that killed the president. Bliss limited Alexander Graham Bell's search to the right side of Garfield's back because he stubbornly assumed that's where the problem lay. He was wrong. The bullet was on the left. Further, Bliss had nothing but contempt for Joseph Lister and his theory about germs. Consequently, he ignorantly searched Garfield's body with dirty utensils and fingers that caused the infection to proliferate and eventually kill the president. In effect, Dr. Bliss, the very physician who assigned himself to help Garfield recover, mortally wounded his patient. As one journalist put it at the time, the physician gave new meaning to the phrase "ignorance is Bliss."

At the risk of sounding brash, I wonder if this intriguing story from history may serve as a parable for us today.

If Dr. Bliss could somehow wave a magic wand and do it all over again, I'd like to think he'd do things differently. I'd like to think he'd be more open to other people's ideas. I'd like to think he'd be more willing to change when he realized what he was doing wasn't working. I'd like to think he'd focus more on the desired outcomes and less on his own familiar methods. And I'd like to think Dr. Bliss could find it within himself to admit that he was part of the problem.

We who are parents, teachers, coaches, employers, or youth workers are informed by the leadership of Dr. D. Willard Bliss. As I lead kids today, I'm reminded of the needless and preventable mistakes this physician made as he cared for James Garfield. I see them in myself. He had the best of intentions, but unfortunately, intentions are not enough. He had no idea of the damage he was doing.

Recently, I was reminded of some common temptations we experience as we lead young people. A high school football coach told me, "I give up. I don't understand these kids, and the school prohibits me from doing what they really need me to do to discipline them. I'm going to finish out my contract this year and go play golf."

Last month, an employer said to me, "I'm frustrated with the interviews I've done with recent college graduates. Last week I had two mothers join their sons for the interview, and they did all the talking. The kids are just not ready for work. So I've decided not to hire any young people. I'm targeting older hires."

A parent heard me talk about this problem and replied, "Dr. Elmore, I know I'm a helicopter parent, and I know it's not good for my kids. They probably need me to stop doing so many things for them. But it feels right to me, and it meets my needs at this point in my life. It's just who I am."

Today, far too many adults have failed their children. We do it unwittingly. We are not bad people, just as Dr. Bliss was not an unqualified physician. He was just blind to what he was doing.

Passion—high.
Self-awareness—low.

How could Dr. Bliss's qualifications be so complete yet his skill set be so incomplete? Actually, we are functioning the same way today. Like Bliss, we find ourselves in a very new and different situation. As Dorothy said to her dog Toto, "We're not in Kansas anymore." No one gave us a manual on how to parent, coach, or teach in the twenty-first century, where technology, culture, and cyberspace play such important roles. But that is where we find ourselves.

In this book, I unveil 12 of the most common mistakes we make as we lead kids today. None of them are deliberate; none are obvious mistakes at first. But every one of them can cripple young people as they grow. I diagnose each mistake, explain why and how it can damage a young person, and furnish some action steps you can take to remedy the error. Finally, I relay a story of a kid who overcame each particular problem and flourished.

A Missing Step in Today's Parenting Path

This past year, I spent countless hours with groups of parents, faculty, coaches, and youth workers. It was eye-opening to say the least. Each conversation became a candid disclosure of the fears, struggles, and preoccupation adults have with today's youth. I made some observations along the way that may prove helpful to you. It became clear that parents and teachers experience various stages as their children and students grow. Their focus shifts from one stage to the next. The shifts are natural, but they can lead to challenges in the relationship—and to mistakes. If you are a parent, recognizing the stages may help you become more self-aware. If you're a teacher, coach, youth worker, or employer, these stages might explain why your young people think and act the way they do.

Stage One: Inspecting

The initial stage in our parenting journey begins at day one. We examine our new baby, bring her home, and begin sizing up her features, traits, and apparent strengths. It's normal for moms and dads to do this. After all, they started the whole thing nine months earlier. Sometimes, however, parents can go nuts, overanalyzing every cough, quirk, twist, and turn. Parents must work to remain balanced.

Too much inspecting can push parents to compare and compete with other families, feeling deficits or advantages in their findings. This can lead to unhealthy distraction from the goal of simply loving and raising a child.

Stage Two: Correcting

Stage two is about our bent to remedy any problems that arise in the first year or two. In fact, this stage doesn't end for years or even decades. Because of their love and concern for their children, parents can get preoccupied with rectifying all wrongs and improving deficient qualities so their children will experience the advantages they deserve. This can lead to obsessive behavior. Moms and dads just want the best for their kids, right?

Too much correcting can make young children feel as though they don't measure up to parents' standards. They can feel inadequate, unloved, or even rejected, causing them to sink into mild cases of depression or melancholy withdrawal from others.

Stage Three: Protecting

At stage three, children have usually begun school, and parents begin focusing on keeping their children safe and secure. They're protecting the investment. This is the first time children are away from their parents for significant lengths of time. It's normal for us to safeguard our kids from harm, but we can go overboard with helmets, knee pads, safety belts, cell phones, and background checks.

Too much protecting can stunt a child's growth. Kids need to experience appropriate levels of risk and failure in order to mature in a healthy way. Too often we prepare the path for the child instead of the child for the path.

Stage Four: Neglecting

When children enter their tween or teen years, they begin to feel like aliens around the house. When parents don't quite know what to do with their "new" kid, they often back off or back down from offering clear leadership. We fear the unknown. We don't ever want to appear uncool, but being hip to culture can cause parents to neglect asking questions they need to be asking.

Too much neglect communicates that we aren't engaged. Kids can misunderstand and confuse our lack of engagement for both ignorance and apathy. Funny—raising these kids was easy when they were young, but now we hardly recognize them. This stage calls for a new kind of leader.

Stage Five: Suspecting

Parents enter stage five as their kids experience adolescence. Their children may have pushed to enter adolescence at eight years old, but now their hormones have caught up. Moms and dads get suspicious about their kids' secrecy or strange new habits and styles. Innocence is replaced by savvy lifestyles and vocabulary. Without a plan, parents and kids divide and separate in this stage of estrangement.

This kind of suspicion can breed distrust. The distrust may be well-deserved, but communication is key during the teen years—even over-communication. Parents must create safe environments to converse and explore a new stage of relationship.

Stage Six: Resurrecting

Finally, as children enter college or show signs of wanting to separate from Mom and Dad's leadership, parents seek to resurrect the relationship at any cost. They want to stay close. They fear losing touch. The distancing is natural for youth, and the clinging may feel natural for adults, but parents must navigate this stage with wisdom. We must not compromise values or identity just to keep life happy.

This is a crucial stage for parents to journey through successfully. When we taught our kids to ride a bike, we blended support with letting go. We must do the same thing at this stage. It's important to relate to kids in a new way and still act as mentors during their young-adult years.

So, What Is Missing?

No doubt, every adult-child relationship is unique. The stages above, however, are remarkably common for caring adults in the home, classroom, or athletic field. For many, an important ingredient is conspicuously absent from these stages, and its absence explains why many teens fail to mature into healthy adults.

What have we left out as we help them mature? After years of inspecting, correcting, protecting, and so on, the natural stage that should follow is *expecting*.

The Missing Step: Expecting

I believe we have under-challenged kids with meaningful work to accomplish. We have overwhelmed them with tests, recitals, and practices, and kids report being stressed-out by these activities. But they are essentially virtual activities. Adults often don't give significant work to students—work that is relevant to life and could actually improve the world if the kids rose to the challenge. We just don't have many expectations of our kids today. Evidently, we assume they're incapable. Instead of rising to our expectations, they drop their heads down to send texts, play video games, scan YouTube clips, and check Facebook postings. Their potential goes untapped. A hundred years ago, 17-year-olds were leading armies, working on the farm, and learning trades as apprentices. Kids could hardly wait to enter the world of adult responsibility. That attitude is rare today.

Here's a thought. Why not talk with your kids and determine what they care deeply about in life. Then offer them a challenge. Whatever their age, expect them to come through and produce something significant. Give them the opportunity to meet great expectations—or better yet, to build great expectations of their own. Invite them into a story that matters.

Author Donald Miller once shared that a friend came to him, grieving that his teenage daughter was dating a guy who was a complete rebel. The kid was a Goth whose lifestyle didn't reflect any of the family's values. In fact, it was both immoral and illegal. Dad didn't know what to do.

Miller simply asked if his friend had considered that his daughter was simply choosing a better story than the one he was creating as a father in his home.

When the man looked puzzled, Miller continued. Everyone wants to be part of a story that is interesting and compelling. They want their life to solve a problem. This man's daughter had simply decided her life at home was boring—and her Goth boyfriend wasn't.

This got Miller's friend to think in new ways. Over the next few months, he did some research and came up with an idea. Over dinner, this father shared about an orphanage in Mexico that desperately needed help. They needed a building, some supplies, and some workers from the United States to accomplish their goals. Dad said he planned to get involved.

In a matter of weeks, his kids were intrigued. His son suggested they visit this orphanage in Mexico, and later, his daughter figured out a way to raise money for it online. Over the next year, this family's story became compelling. Eventually, the teenage daughter approached her father and told him she'd broken up with her boyfriend. She said she couldn't believe she was even attracted to him in the first place. Needless to say, Dad was elated.

Hmm…I think I know why she didn't need the guy anymore. She found a better story at home.

Here's to expecting something significant from life and from our kids. Here's to creating stories that pull the very best out of them. Even more, here's to avoiding the mistakes and pitfalls that prevent kids from reaching their potential.

We Won't Let Them Fail

When my son, Jonathan, was very young, we did what many dads and sons do. We played whiffle ball out in our yard. Jonathan has a number of talents, but we soon discovered baseball is not one. He may be the next Steve Jobs or Walt Disney, but he was no Josh Hamilton or Derek Jeter when it came to hitting a ball. So I found myself making it easier and easier. I got closer to him and threw the ball slower to ensure he'd finally succeed. After some time, he finally hit it. (I wondered if I might have to go inside and shave again it took so long.) I'm pretty sure it was an accident.

We both celebrated the hit, and then he wanted to try some more. Since we had a good thing going, I didn't want him to fail. So I made it impossible for him to fail. I made hitting the ball so easy, it might as well have been a T-ball.

That season, we signed him up to play T-ball. It was a comedy. He stood in the outfield, staring at his mitt or at the sky, his imagination wandering through space—even when a ball was hit to him. It just wasn't his thing. Yet I didn't want him to fail at this game I loved so much, so I just kept making it easier and easier.

It finally caught up with me—and with him. All the extra steps I took to make it impossible for him to fail were appropriate when he was four or five years old. They were not appropriate as he moved into the fourth grade. I discovered I'd given him some unrealistic expectations and false assumptions by not allowing him to experience life as it really was. He thought he was good at baseball—and drew laughter from classmates when they actually saw him play. It was then we had a heart-to-heart talk.

I'll be the first to admit this was not the end of the world. It is, however, a picture of how I learned to correct a mistake. Every parent and teacher wants to see their kids succeed in school, in sports, and in life, but making it impossible to fail isn't the answer. Removing failure, in fact, is a terrific way to stunt maturity. A recent survey of young MBA students revealed that Generation iY (those born after 1990) is actually begging adults to let them explore and fail. A top response from the survey said they want to *learn to fail—quickly*. Waiting on this lesson makes it harder.

We Fail When We Don't Let Them Fail

Far too often, adults intuitively feel we will ruin our children's self-esteem if we let them fail. They need to feel special—to believe they are winners—and we assume this means we can't let them fail. Actually, the opposite is true. Genuine, healthy self-esteem develops when caring adults identify children's strengths but also allow them the satisfaction that comes only from trying and failing. Effort, failure, and eventual triumph builds great emerging adults. Unfortunately, for too long we've failed them.

- As parents, we've given them lots of possessions but not much perspective.

- As educators, we've given them plenty of schools but not plenty of skills.

- As coaches, we've taught them how to win games but not how to win in life.

- As youth workers, we provide lots of explanations but not enough experiences.

- As employers, we've mentored them in profit and loss but haven't shown them how to profit from loss.

It's time our leadership caught up with their needs. Kids are growing up in a very different world from the one we grew up in. Teachers, coaches, and parents have changed the way they approach leading students. Some of these changes are great, but some have had unintended consequences.

Why Adults Won't Let Kids Fail

The shift seems to have started more than 30 years ago with the Tylenol scare in September 1982. Do you remember that? Bottles of Tylenol had been poisoned and were removed from drugstore shelves everywhere. The next month, as kids trick-or-treated at strangers' homes, adults seemed to rise up, launch hotlines, and determine we would safeguard our kids from harm. In the years following this incident, it was as though America turned her attention to the children.

Safety wasn't the only issue. By the 1990s, we had determined to boost self-esteem and ensure kids grew up confident and comfortable in this very uncertain world. Diaper-changing tables in public restrooms now signal that these kids are a top priority. Baby on Board signs on minivans in the 1990s led to bumper stickers that read My Kid Is a Super Kid, or My Kid Made the Honor Roll. When they play soccer or Little League baseball, every kid gets a trophy, win or lose, just for being on the team. Kids' bedrooms are lined with ribbons and awards, and they've never won a championship.

Next, we determined to give our kids a head start in everything they did. We came to believe that all caring parents should use Baby Einstein and Baby Mozart with their young children. We wanted to give our kids a decided advantage, an edge on their peers, because ours are so special. I agree with promoting self-esteem, assuring safety, applauding participation, and providing head starts, but I believe we've given kids a false sense of reality. We've set them up for a painful wake-up call as they grow older. Social scientists agree that our emphasis on winning has produced highly confident kids. Sadly, they also agree that this ill-prepares them for the world that awaits them.

Think about the unintended consequences of these changes I've described. Many middle-class kids have never experienced significant setbacks. And often they are unprepared to navigate them as they reach their twenties. For example, in the past, when a student got in trouble or failed a class, parents reinforced the teacher's grade and insisted their children study harder. The children learned, *I failed, but the adults around me believe I can get back up, try again, and succeed.* When that same situation occurs today, parents often side with their children, and the teacher gets in trouble. The child learns, *I will soon be out of this mess because the adults around me will make excuses and not let me fail.*

Hmm…why do we do this? Let me suggest one reason. Moms and dads frequently turn their children into their trophies. They see their children as reflections of their own success. Every kid is a winner so Mom and Dad can be winners too. We look better. There's no mess.

And parents are not the only culprits. Educators have done the same thing. We pass kids on to the next grade even if they're not really ready for it. We graduate them even if they didn't legitimately pass a class so our school can get the federal funding we deserve. In colleges, pushing students toward a degree helps the statistics on retention and graduation. Once again, we see our students as reflections of us and our achievements. This is poor preparation for their future.

Recently, a school district superintendent asked me for some advice on handling a situation he'd never faced before. He told me some of his schools were no longer using red ink to grade papers. Why? It was too harsh for the students. It caused too much stress. Two high schools wanted to do away with grades and class levels all together. They felt it was damaging to have distinctions like freshmen, sophomores, juniors, and seniors. Parents and teachers suggested some of the teens who were 18 but still sophomores felt belittled and behind.

Have we forgotten this is not how life works after childhood? I hate to see students discouraged, but removing the opportunity to fail is not the solution. These kids feel behind because they *are* behind. Perhaps the best motivation to get them moving is to equip them to face reality with tenacity. What they need most are adults who actually believe they can do it—and who provide support and accountability until they do. Sooner or later, they'll have to perform.

This belief that we cannot let kids fail has gone international. A few years ago, the Professional Association of Teachers in England suggested even the thought of failure was damaging to students. Liz Beattie, a retired teacher, called on the association's annual gathering in Buxton, Derbyshire, to "delete the word 'fail' from the educational vocabulary, to be replaced with the concept of 'deferred success.'" Again, I have to wonder if this is genuinely helpful or if adults are simply in denial.

The good news is, not everyone is buying it, including United Kingdom Education Secretary Ruth Kelly.

> For that particular proposal, I think I'd give them 0 out of 10. It's really important for young people to grow up with the ability to get on and achieve, but also to find out what failure is. When young people grow up and enter the adult world, they have to deal with success and failure, and education is about creating well-rounded young people who can deal with these sorts of situations.[1]

Our problem is, we assume our kids are too fragile. Many of us adults just don't believe our kids are capable of failing and then getting back up and moving forward. Instead, we assume we can just talk to them about commonsense items like safe driving, job hunting, breaking up, or hosting parties. Dr. Michael Ungar, a child therapist, says it doesn't work that way.

> We seem these days to have a magical notion that children can learn common sense by just watching and listening to others talk about it. That just isn't the way our brains develop. We are experiential beings. Lev Vygotsky, a famous child psychologist from Russia, demonstrated very well what he calls "zones of proximal development." We need to be pushed, not too far, but just enough to learn something new. Good development occurs when we are invited to accept challenges that are just big enough to demand we work at solving them, but that they don't completely defeat us.[2]

I believe this includes failure.

Consider this fact. Over the years our families have gotten smaller.

We've been able to provide much better care for our children. It's allowed us to pay much more attention to our kids and their self-actualization. Unfortunately, we began to assume that if we really care for these young people, we shouldn't let them fail, fall, fear, or fight. Instead, we will nurture them, keep them safe from all harm, and ensure they are happy as they leave our schools and homes. In short, we made life easy and removed nearly every opportunity to grow strong through struggle and failure.

The Consequences of Refusing to Let Them Fail

Refusing to let kids fail brings two negative outcomes. First, it fosters the fear of failure later in life as adults. Having never mastered it as a child, it becomes a master when the stakes are high. Second, it dilutes the will or motivation to excel.

─────────────── THE PRINCIPLE ───────────────
Removing the possibility of failure dilutes
the motivation to excel.

Let me illustrate these consequences with a simple analogy. During the past two decades, much playground equipment has been removed from public parks. Adults, especially parents, have worried about children falling down and getting hurt or breaking a bone, so they demanded the monkey bars or jungle gyms be taken down.

This makes sense if we're concerned only about today. Sadly, we've begun to see the unintended by-product of this safety measure. John Tierney reported in the *New York Times* that researchers now question the value of safety-first playgrounds.

> Even if children do suffer fewer physical injuries—and the evidence for that is debatable—the critics say that these playgrounds may stunt emotional development, leaving children with anxieties and fears that are ultimately worse than a broken bone.

"Children need to encounter risks and overcome fears on the playground," said Ellen Sandseter, professor of psychology at Queen Maud University in Norway. "I think monkey bars and tall slides are great. As playgrounds become more and more boring, these are some of the few features that still can give children thrilling experiences with heights and high speed."

After studying kids on playgrounds in Norway, England and Australia, Dr. Sandseter identified six categories of risky play: exploring heights, experiencing high speed, handling dangerous tools, being near dangerous elements (like fire or water), rough-and-tumble play (like wrestling), and wandering alone away from adult supervision...

"Climbing equipment needs to be high enough, or else it will be too boring in the long run," Dr. Sandseter said. "Children approach thrills and risks in a progressive manner, and very few children would try to climb to the highest point for the first time they climb. The best thing is to let children encounter these challenges from an early age, and they will then progressively learn to master them through their play over the years."

Sometimes, of course, their mastery fails, and falls are the common form of playground injury. But these rarely cause permanent damage, either physically or emotionally...A child who's hurt in a fall before the age of 9 is less likely as a teenager to have a fear of heights...

By gradually exposing themselves to more and more dangers on a playground, children are using the same habituation techniques developed by therapists to help adults conquer phobias, according to Dr. Sandseter and a fellow psychologist, Leif Kennair..."Paradoxically, we posit that our fear of children being harmed by mostly harmless injuries may result in more fearful children and increased levels of psychopathology."[3]

Helping Kids Fail Well

John Killinger said, "Failure is the greatest opportunity to know who I really am." I have come to believe that failure is not only *normal* for those who ultimately succeed—it is *necessary*. Dr. Joyce Brothers suggests, "The person interested in success has to learn to view failure as a healthy, inevitable part of the process of getting to the top." Let's examine three steps we must take to help kids fail well.

We must create a safe place to fail.

I worked under John C. Maxwell for more than two decades. He taught me this lesson over and over again. In his book *Failing Forward*, he relates the story of an art teacher who performed an experiment with two classes of students. It is a parable on the benefits of failure.

> The ceramics teacher announced on opening day that he was dividing the class into two groups. All those on the left side of the studio, he said, would be graded solely on the quantity of work produced, while all those on the right side on its quality. His procedure was simple: on the final day of class he would bring in his bathroom scales and weigh the work of the "quantity" group: fifty pounds rated an "A", forty pounds a "B" and so on. Those being graded on "quality," however, needed to produce only one pot— albeit a perfect one—to get an "A." Well, at grading time a curious fact emerged: the works of the highest quality were all produced by the group being graded for quantity. It seems that while the "quantity" group was busily churning out piles of work—and learning from their mistakes—the "quality" group had sat theorizing about perfection, and in the end had little more to show for their efforts than grandiose theories and a pile of dead clay.[4]

This illustrates our natural disposition. When people—especially young people—know they are free to try something and fail, their performance usually improves. It brings out the best in them. But if they are preoccupied with trying not to fail, they become paralyzed.

In 1933, the crew building the Golden Gate Bridge fell behind on the deadlines. One of the workers had fallen to his death, causing his colleagues to work more slowly each day for fear of it happening again. Finally, one worker approached the supervisor and asked if a net could be placed underneath the men to save them if they fell. The supervisor was apprehensive to take the time to do this because they were already behind schedule. But he eventually agreed, and a net was hoisted into position. Suddenly, the men worked faster and more efficiently— actually speeding up the completion of the bridge. What enabled them to work faster and better? Removing the fear of failure. Suddenly, it was safe to try what they had feared before.

We must help them see the benefits of failing.

Once we create environments where kids feel safe to fail, we must encourage them to embrace it. Failure is part of growing up and succeeding. Adults need to help them see the advantages of failure. But just what are the benefits of failure? When we handle it well, failure has these advantages:

Failure can create resilience. When a student realizes that failure isn't fatal, she begins to build resilience from within. Just as lifting weights builds physical muscles, pushing back against failure builds emotional muscles. Kids learn to bounce back quickly and try new options to succeed.

Failure can force us to evaluate. Once students overcome the initial discouragement of failing at a goal, they're forced to assess what happened. This is a huge benefit. Why did their attempt fail? What could they do better? Immediate success blinds us to ways to improve.

Failure can motivate us to better performance. If a child grows up in an environment where failure is safe, it actually becomes a source of motivation, not despair. It stimulates and inspires greater effort. As a kid playing baseball, failure provoked me to get back out there and try again.

Failure prompts creativity and discovery. Perhaps a majority of the inventions during the twentieth century were results of initial failures— think of Edison, Bell, and Oppenheimer. It sounds cliché, but failure is a teacher that guides us to greater insight and innovation…if we'll learn from it.

Failure can develop maturity. Best of all, authentic maturity happens only when we deal with failure well. If I developed any virtues growing up, such as patience, empathy, sacrifice, or tenacity, it was because I learned to regard failure as a friend.

We must help them make failure their best friend.

Benjamin Franklin said, "The things which hurt, instruct." Your *attitude* toward failure determines your *altitude* after failure. The same is true for students. What they allow to reside in their minds makes all the difference. I think Warren Wiersbe was right when he said, "A realist is an idealist who has gone through the fire and been purified. A skeptic is an idealist who has gone through the fire and been burned."

My friend Kyle Stark develops young men for a living. He is the assistant general manager for the Pittsburgh Pirates. Having watched teenagers enter professional baseball, he makes this observation:

> Failure separates those who think they want success from those who are determined to win. Failure narrows the playing field. The first people out are those who blame others. Next out are those who lost interest. The weak go first. The strong learn to hang in there and keep bouncing back until they win.
>
> The thin-skinned rarely win due to brittle egos and apprehensive attitudes. Thick skin comes from falling and failing. The falls produce wounds that heal and reveal a connection between resilience and a peculiar resolve that accepts failure as a temporary condition. They accept both good and bad so they don't forfeit the blessing of learning from both.
>
> The thick-skinned prepare to win by increasingly expanding their willingness to endure pain in affirming the degree of true desire. They allow every challenge to serve as an opportunity to changes for the better. They continue to learn that bitterness is poison and quickly purge its deadly

influence on their endurance and desire. They see a prize in every problem and potential in every person. They see their faults but never focus on them. They know that whatever is on the mind will eventually get in the mind. The power of positive word choice determines each choice of the next deed. Wasting time talking about everything that cannot change and about nothing that can is pointless.[5]

Stop Cheating Them

So what can we do? Try this. Identify experiences in which you'll allow young people to take calculated risks and experience failure, such as a project or class. Coach them but don't intervene and do the work for them. Help them build emotional muscles that are capable of enduring a failure. Allow them to know from experience that there is still life after failure.

When my son, Jonathan, was a teenager, he double booked himself on the calendar. He asked if I'd call his supervisor and negotiate it for him. I said, "JC, I'd love to, but that won't help you in the long run. I want you to call and determine a win/win solution." He made the call and lived to tell about it. And he now knows how to do it.

Dr. Ungar challenges parents to give their kids the risk taker's advantage.

> I'd rather a child ride his bicycle on a busy street and learn how to respect traffic before he gets behind the wheel of a car. I'd rather a child do crazy stunts on the monkey bars at age four, and on his BMX bike at the extreme skateboard park when he is 14 (even if there is a risk of a broken bone), if it means he won't be doing stupid things with his body when he is 24 (like experimenting with excessive drugs or drinking). I'd rather an 8-year-old choose his own friends and suffer the consequences of being taken advantage of or emotionally hurt while his parents are still there to talk with him about it, rather than waiting until he is an ill-prepared 18-year-old who arrives at a college dorm

completely unprepared for the complex relationships he'll navigate as a new student.[6]

Billy was a kid who grew up in such an environment. His parents worried about his social awkwardness in school and his tendency to withdraw, but they continued to encourage him to explore all kinds of ideas to discover what he wanted to do with his life after high school. They made it safe to fail. And fail he did. I'm glad he did—we all have benefited from the success that ultimately followed his failures as a businessman. His name is Bill Gates.

As a 13-year old kid, Bill had already shown an interest in early versions of the computer. From the proceeds of a rummage sale at Lakeside School, his mother suggested they purchase a Teletype terminal for the kids, hoping that this might nudge her son from boredom to passion. It worked.

In the years that followed, however, Bill experienced a number of failures. He was a social outsider, not well connected to others in college. He spent more time in the computer lab than in class and eventually dropped out. He and his partner, Paul Allen, started an initial company called Traf-O-Data that revealed traffic patterns in Seattle. It was considered a failure, and they dropped it. But in an environment where it was safe to fail, Bill continued unwavering, soon launching Microsoft, and the rest is history. He is now one of the richest and most generous men in the world.

The fact is, failure almost always precedes success.

Do we consider Michael Jordan a failure? He stated, "I've missed more than 9000 shots in my career. I've lost almost 300 games. Twenty-six times I've been trusted to take the game-winning shot and missed. I've failed over and over and over again in my life. And that is why I succeed."

We Project Our Lives on Them

On a warm, sunny summer day, I was in Iowa preparing to speak to educators. As I drove past some ball fields to my hotel, I saw a Little League baseball game in progress. Although I knew none of the kids or parents, I decided to stop to watch for a while. For me, watching baseball at any level is therapeutic.

What I watched that day was a clinic on parenting—or rather, on unhealthy parenting. Have you seen a kids' sports league in action lately? Whether it's soccer, football, basketball, or whatever, parents can be the number one headache for referees, umpires, coaches, and kids. On this day, I saw it played out vividly.

One tiny eight-year-old boy stepped up to the plate. Before settling into the batter's box, he peered down the line at the third base coach. The stocky man, middle-aged and balding, was clapping his hands firmly as if to project confidence to the small boy. Seconds afterward, the first pitch came in. The kid swung at it recklessly and missed. Strike one. The second and third pitches came in almost exactly as the first one did—with the same results. The boy struck out on three pitches.

Ugh. I felt badly, not even knowing the poor kid. Yet I didn't feel half as badly as the little player and that third base coach. Immediately, the stocky, balding man began yelling at the top of his lungs at the kid, swearing at him for striking out. "What the #*@*! were you swinging at up there? I can't believe what I just saw! Get over to the #*$@#!* dugout and think about what you just did. You are a sorry #%$*@&* excuse for a ballplayer."

With shoulders slumped and almost in tears, that pitiful little boy tucked his tail between his legs and crawled into the dugout. He was embarrassed in front of two dozen peers and about a hundred adults. The kid was eight years old. I soon learned the third base coach was his father.

I couldn't believe my ears. How could this dad yell at his second-grader so violently? I certainly understand the need for kids to learn to focus, practice, and work hard in competitions. But his reaction was over the top. Part of me wanted to run down onto the field, grab this man by the shoulders, look him in the eye and say, "Do you realize what you're doing? The chances of your kid going pro in baseball are likely .03 percent. You're screaming at a future software developer. Furthermore, the only reason I can think of that you'd take this game so seriously is that you're fat and 40 and can't play ball anymore yourself, so you've chosen to live out your unlived life through your son."

Fortunately for everyone, I didn't do that, and the game went on. The next time that kid stepped up to hit, he was less confident than before. He was in fear. But in Little League baseball games, the tide can turn quickly. When a pitch came in over the plate, this same eight-year-old boy swung and hit the ball, and off he ran to first base. (These things happen.) The good news for Little Leaguers is that when you hit a ball, you can often keep running because few players can actually catch or field a hard-hit ball. The boy kept rounding the bases until finally he was heading for home. He slid into home plate just ahead of the throw. It was amazing. This kid who struck out in his last time at bat had just hit a home run.

As soon as he rose from the dirt, he looked down the third base line to see what his dad would say or do. This time, we all watched the man, standing in the third base coach's box, waving for the boy to come over to him. He then spread out his arms as his boy ran toward him, as if to say, "This time you performed well. Come and get your hug."

Reflect for a moment on what this dad was unwittingly communicating to his son on that day. "First, if you mess up, beware. I'll be yelling and swearing at you to get your act together. I'll even stoop to intimidation and embarrassment. Second, if you perform well, you get my affection and approval. You are acceptable. But all my love and attention depends upon your performance."

Hmm...do you think that just maybe this poor boy may grow up with some unhealthy emotions? I don't claim to be a psychological guru, but even a cursory understanding of kids' hearts and minds teaches us that this isn't the way to help them succeed. Based on our qualitative research, most parents agree with that statement. So why do so many of us find ourselves becoming so emotional when it comes to our children? Further, why do we frequently react emotionally to our kids? Why do we commonly take our frustrations out on them?

Making the Grade

Not long ago, I spoke to two middle school principals. Their schools are not geographically close, but they told me the same story. Both relayed how the mother of one of their students had marched into their office in a rage. The two moms were angry over the poor grade their child had received on a paper. Each of the principals sat down with the parents, and in a civil manner, attempted to explain the red ink on the paper. In both cases, the teachers joined them in the conversation.

As the discussion evolved, both principals smiled as they shared with me their surprise at how familiar these parents were with their kid's paper. They seemed to know every page and line on that paper. It slowly dawned on each principal what had happened—the parents had actually written the paper for their child. It's no wonder they were angry. *They* had received a bad grade for their work.

The bottom line is this. Whether it's a sports team or a classroom, many moms and dads are living vicariously through their children. We are determined to make sure our kids make their mark, even if it means making it for them. Why? Because our children are ultimately a reflection on us. They represent our second chance to get it right. Through them we may get to do our childhood over again.

You might think I'm exaggerating, but for hundreds of thousands of parents, this issue remains the number one problem in raising healthy kids. If we still have our own unresolved issues, how can we ever expect to develop healthy young people at home?

In a nutshell, when we project our lives on our kids, they often feel pressured to become something they are not. Consider stories you've heard over the years. It's the son who feels forced to go into the family business even though he has no passion or gifts for it. It's the daughter who feels compelled to excel at gymnastics because mom wanted to as a young girl, and it never panned out for her. It's the child who is pushed excessively hard to make an A in science because Dad or Mom never did, and doggone it, they plan to get a good grade this time around. The truth be told, science may not come naturally for either the parents or the child.

— THE PRINCIPLE —
When adults project, they pressure kids to
become someone they are not.

Let's face it. We used to laugh when we heard about dads yelling at umpires during Little League baseball games. We laughed when mothers went crazy and attacked their daughter's "frenemy" on the cheerleading squad. We laughed at "stage moms" who went ballistic when their son or daughter didn't get the role they wanted in the school play. But now incidents like these are increasing, so we don't know whether to laugh or cry. Here's my question. Don't these sound like accounts of adults acting like children? I believe that parental projection—living vicariously through our children—explains at least some of this behavior.

The Unintended Consequences

Let me summarize the unintended outcomes of projecting on our children.

We fail to model healthy behavior that kids can emulate.

Healthy lifestyles are more caught than taught. Regardless of the important things you hope to say to your children or do for your children, none of them are more important than the life you live in front of your children. People do what people see. In the words of Albert Schweitzer, "Example is everything."

We create stress in them, forcing them to become someone they're not.

When we project, children are eventually motivated not by their own gifts or identity but by ours. That's never healthy. Their quiet ambition is to not disappoint the adults in their lives rather than to pursue their own dreams. Even if their effort looks like healthy ambition at first, it catches up to them and creates emotional sickness.

Our relationship with them becomes strained and unhealthy.

Because both the parent and the child are acting out of wrong motives, both parties become emotionally unhealthy, and the connection between parent and child is strained. As the child becomes an adult, holidays are difficult, conversations are awkward, and any shared activity can feel forced. No one looks forward to the interaction—the child feels inadequate, and the parent feels disappointed.

Your Motivation Impacts Their Motivation

We live in a bottom-line, result-oriented culture. All of our lives we've been told to make the grade, make the team, make the money, make the sale, make a difference. None of these ambitions are wrong, but with unhealthy motives, we can fall into a performance trap. As adults, we may feel this from our past, and if we do, we most assuredly will pass it on to our kids unless we're careful.

Years ago, I taught college students in San Diego, California. Michael, a senior, began to struggle during the fall semester, and I could tell he needed a break. I later found out Michael was under all kinds of pressure with a full load of classes, a part-time job, a girlfriend, two big leadership responsibilities on campus, and a dad breathing down his neck to make good grades. He began seeing a counselor, who didn't take long to summarize Michael's dilemma. She simply said, "Your problem is, you've become a 'human doing' before you've allowed yourself to be a 'human being.'"

Sadly, this is true of so many today. We are human doings. Our identity is completely tied to our performance. If this sounds familiar, you may have picked it up from your parents and are now contagious with your own children. It's a pattern, an unhealthy cycle. It can create a lifestyle of unhappiness, leaving kids feeling trapped by adults. In short, if kids feel forced to do something, their intrinsic satisfaction can fade, and with it, their fulfillment, their passion, and their ambition.

The Reward Experiment

I spoke with author Daniel Pink last month about this very reality. He reminded me of a school experiment in which preschool students were divided into three groups. Group 1 was the Expected Reward group. They were told that when they drew a picture, they'd get a reward. The second was called the Unexpected Reward group. They were not told about the reward up front, but when they drew a picture, they got one. The third group of kids was called the No Reward group. Researchers asked these kids if they wanted to draw but didn't promise a reward at the beginning or give them one at the end. As all three groups drew their pictures, the researchers followed through. The first two groups got a prize. The third group did not, and those kids never saw what the first two groups received.

Two weeks later, they performed this exercise again. This time, the first group was asked if they wanted to draw a picture, but unlike the first time, they were told they would not get any prizes. Interestingly, no kid in the first group wanted to draw much anymore. The second two groups—neither of which was told about a reward—drew just as much as they did the first time and with the same delight.

The researchers' conclusion was simple but profound. In the beginning, the students enjoyed drawing pictures, but as the motivation became external rather than internal, they lost their zeal unless they were rewarded.[1] It was all about the prize or about pleasing an adult. Think about it—adults experience the same reality. Life often becomes about external rewards or punishments. Carrots and sticks. We lose the joy of simply doing a job we love. And when we feel something is imposed on us, we often dig in our heels and lose our internal drive. At times, we even rebel. The strongest motivation always comes from the inside, when a child has three things:

- *Autonomy.* "I can do it on my own, at my own pace."
- *Mastery.* "I feel like I am growing and improving."
- *Purpose.* "I do this because it's meaningful to me."[2]

Even when you believe you're pushing kids in the right direction, if they perform only for you, the experience becomes sour. Adults who pressure kids to do or become something often steal the true motivation those kids should feel as they perform. If the rewards are all external, kids will require consistent external pushes to continue. But if we allow them to find their own passions, gifts, and calling, the reward will become the very satisfaction of the task itself. The energy comes from internal ambition, not external stimuli—healthy or unhealthy. (More on this later.)

Diagnosing the Problem

Let's examine the symptoms of young people who are motivated externally—by adults imposing their wishes on the child. How do they tend to cope? Explore the chart below. Each child has inward needs that require attention. As parents, if we fail to address these needs in healthy ways, our kids may begin to compensate for their insecurities. They'll want to balance out their inadequacies. Personal security is essential to living a healthy life.

Inner need	If missing, they feel…	Common symptoms
belonging	insecure	overcompensation, emotional highs and lows
worth	inferior	competition, self-doubt, need for recognition
competence	inadequate	comparison with specific people, defensive attitude
purpose	insignificant	compulsive, driven spirit, defeat, depression

More kids today struggle with depression and anxiety than at any time in modern history. According to Dr. Madeline Levine, author of *The Price of Privilege*, America's newly defined at-risk group is pre-teens and teens from affluent, well-educated families. In spite of their economic and social advantages, they experience the highest rates of depression, substance abuse, anxiety disorders, and unhappiness of any group of children in this country. Adolescent suicide has quadrupled since 1950.[3]

When I discovered this, I decided to do some qualitative research with the tens of thousands of students we work with each year at Growing Leaders. I discovered that more than 80 percent of these emotional disorders are induced by well-intentioned parents who project on their kids. By living vicariously through their kids, they send a negative message to their children. The children believe they haven't measured up to their parents' wishes. The parental pressure makes them feel is if they've disappointed Dad or Mom and must now find a way to make their parents feel better and make up for their own inadequacies. These are some of the most popular coping mechanisms.

* *Comparison.* They compare themselves to their siblings. The motivation is horizontal and external.

- *Compensation.* They feel like victims and try to compensate by excusing their inferiority.

- *Condemnation.* They become judgmental of themselves or others, trying to fix the blame.

- *Competition.* They feel they lost the "please my parents" game and compete somewhere else, where they can win.

- *Compulsion.* They perform compulsively to gain their parents' approval, eventually becoming people-pleasers.

THINK IT OVER

Sadly, as kids resort to these coping mechanisms, they begin to find their identity in something besides who they were created to be. Do your children exhibit any of these symptoms? Do you have reason to suspect they might be in a performance trap?

How to Correct This Mistake

Let me suggest some action steps you can take to remedy this mistake.

Model a healthy identity yourself.

A trend is growing among adults today. We are modeling poor behavior for our children, and that explains why kids are acting the way they are. According to the Associated Press, it's *adults* who bully. "Half the employers in a 2011 survey by the management association reported incidents of bullying in their workplace."[4] Let's face it. Emotional health and maturity often has little to do with age. We teach what we know, but we reproduce what we are. The surest way to raise healthy sons and daughters is to ensure we are emotionally healthy ourselves.

Expose, don't impose.

One of our greatest temptations as parents may be to direct all of our kids' activities, even as they enter their teen years. Instead of imposing our ideas, what if we chose to expose them to ideas, people, and places and then let them choose what to do? I did this with my kids and found that once they missed a great opportunity, they didn't want to miss any others. I let them decide whether to be involved. What's more, before you suggest any activity for your kids, STOP. Ask yourself if it fits their…

- *Style.* Kids have their own identity. It's tied to yours, but it is nevertheless unique.
- *Talent.* Your kids have their own special talents. They are different from yours.
- *Opportunity.* Kids should feel opportunities are natural, not forced.
- *Passion.* Kids have their own set of interests. They are likely to love things you don't and vice versa.

Communicate that your love for them is not tied to their performance.

Be sure you consistently show your kids and tell your kids that you love them and approve of them regardless of whether they like the things you like. Even more importantly, tell them and show them that your love for them is not based on whether they are good at the things you enjoy. My children were not interested in sports, so I had to make sure they didn't feel as if that disappointed me. I just learned to love what they loved, and I put my personal love of sports on the back burner for a few seasons.

Help them align their identity with their activity.

Your children have their own purpose in life. It may or may not overlap with yours. You gave birth to them, but they have their own unique set of cards in their hand and must play them. You can help, but as they mature, they must discover who they are and what they must do. The best way you can help them is to observe where their passions and strengths lie and then align that identity to the activities they engage in each week. As they age, your role will change from supervisor to consultant. Parents must help their kids find their...

- *Interests*—what preoccupies them and the activities they're passionate about.
- *Strengths*—what they are very good at doing, where they excel.
- *Burdens*—what moves them with empathy and compassion.
- *Expertise*—what they know a lot about and how they can add value to others.
- *Influence*—where they exercise the most influence with people.

Offer them the blessing.

In various cultures, the *blessing* is a rite-of-passage ceremony as youth transition from childhood to adulthood. This blessing is a gift—an adult imparts belief and acceptance to the youth. Historically, it involved fathers speaking timely, affirming words to their children. We see this modeled in Scripture as Isaac blessed Jacob (Genesis 27) and Jacob spoke to his sons (Genesis 49). Those who fall into performance traps frequently strive for the approval of someone they admire—often a father figure (someone in authority). Kids feel an internal need for someone to recognize their uniqueness and affirm it out loud. When adults who love them speak words of positive affirmation, children hear that they have what it takes. Confidence and peace are the result.

What I'm Not Talking About

When I warn against projecting our lives on our children, I'm not saying we shouldn't share our stories with our kids. There's a huge difference between sharing our stories or life lessons with them and imposing our unrealized dreams on them, hoping they'll fulfill those dreams for our sake. A growing body of research suggests that kids, whether young children or adolescents, actually benefit emotionally and psychologically from knowing the stories from their heritage.

> From the moment of birth, children are surrounded by stories—stories of themselves, their parents, and their parents before them. Indeed over 90 percent of parents report that they tell family stories to their infants, well before their infants are able to participate in understanding or telling these stories themselves.[5] Stories are a powerful frame for understanding the world and the self.[6] Who we are is largely defined by the experiences we have had and how we understand those experiences.[7] There is growing evidence in the psychological literature that narratives of one's own personal experiences are critical for identity and wellbeing. Individuals who are able to create more coherent and emotionally expressive narratives about stressful events subsequently show lower levels of depression and anxiety.[8]

As our children grew up, we spent some of our mealtimes sharing family stories in a game we called Did You Know…Our son and daughter heard about how their grandparents met, how their uncle would sleepwalk, how I got my first job, how Mom and Dad got engaged, and how I failed so often along the way. (For some reason, they loved the stories about failure. Imagine that.)

Remember the Fences

My son, Jonathan, turned 21 last year. Recently I told my friend Steve about a talk I had with Jonathan about the life stage he's entering—a stage that feels strange because of his transition from child to adult. Steve immediately reminded me of a metaphor our mutual mentor, Keith Drury, used that explains it simply.

All good parents erect fences for their children as they grow up. The fences surround the children and protect them. These fences are the values that moms and dads relay to their kids, either by default or by design. Parents do this for the purpose of safety, guidance, and boundaries. The fences prevent the children from wandering too far off the right path and making poor decisions. The boundaries vary from family to family, but most moms and dads provide these fences to their kids. After all, their parents did the same thing for them as they grew up.

Some parents fail to realize that it's the job of every child to tear down their parents' fence and build their own. Yep, you read that right. At some point, the child must construct her own fence. It isn't that Mom's fence is bad, it's simply that every emerging adult must own her own fence. There are few more pitiful scenarios than a 30-year-old who still lives at home and cannot navigate his own decisions. Or worse, a man in a midlife crisis because he suddenly decides he wants to adjust his fence. Regardless of where children's fences are located, they must be their own fences by the time they become adults. If they simply continue using their parents' fences as adults, the fences will likely get knocked down the first time someone pushes against them because they weren't their own. This happens in college far too many times.

All parents hope that their kids build fences very close to the spot where their parents' fences are located. But most of the time, the fence goes up in a little different place. It's natural. Parents, teachers, coaches, and youth workers must recognize this and *control their desire to control*. If Mom and Dad can transition from the role of supervisor to consultant during this process, they actually increase the chances that their children will build fences near and similar to their own.

Three Temptations for Parents

Adults can fall into at least three traps as they provide fences for their children.

Neglecting. Some parents fail to provide clear fences for their children. In the interest of being hip or relevant (or at least not antiquated), some parents never build fences for their kids growing up. They don't want their kids to feel boxed in or other parents to think they're uncool. Eventually those kids become brats, or worse, they're influenced by every whim or trend that others impose on them. They have no compass in life. Today, millions of moms and dads neglect to provide fences for their kids. As a result, their children grow up insecure and don't know how to build their own fences. They never saw one at home.

Imposing. Other parents make a different mistake. They continue to impose their fences on their grown children long after their sons or daughters should have built their own. They nag, push, intimidate, or withhold money or affection to get their kids to do exactly as they wish. They want to remain in control of the boundaries. I understand this predisposition, but it usually comes back to bite both the parent and the son or daughter. It creates an awkward relationship that's built on manipulation rather than trust. The children become unhealthy adults—even emotionally disabled.

Confusing. A third mistake occurs too often when faith plays an important role in the family. Families can confuse the parents' fence with God's fence. Stop and reflect on this for a moment. Mom and Dad may say to their 15-year-old daughter, "Be home by ten o'clock." That's a fair rule, but it's a fence Mom and Dad created. It isn't God's fence. There is no Scripture verse that says to be home by ten. There is, on the other hand, a passage that instructs children to respect their parents. *That's* God's fence. But there is a difference. Parents must not impose or inflict a rule as if it were divine. We must not confuse our children by hinting that our rules are straight from heaven.

I've worked with high school and college students for decades, and I have seen the damage that alcohol can do, so our family has never been drinkers. I don't condemn it for others; I've just chosen to not keep liquor in the house. This choice is one I've tried to explain to my children without making them feel I'm imposing it on them as adults or pushing a legalistic code of conduct.

Recently, my 24-year-old daughter decided to keep some wine in the refrigerator and have a glass from time to time. I am now experiencing a new fence as a dad. I obviously want her to drink responsibly. My hope is that she continues to see me model wisdom and yet, at the same time, not feel judged because her fence isn't located where mine is. It's not easy.

The Tools We Must Provide

This is why it's paramount for caring adults not only to furnish fences and then allow kids to build their own, but also to teach them *how* to build their own fences when the time comes. We do this by providing them with a handful of tools.

Models. We must model a lifestyle we hope our children want to embrace. No words can replace an example. We can't expect kids to live by standards we have not adopted. And if it doesn't work at home, we have no right to export it.

Worldview. We must help our kids construct a framework that enables them to make good decisions. A worldview is a lens that helps them perceive and understand the world. It's a grid that furnishes them with the big picture.

Critical thinking. Next we must teach our kids to evaluate the culture around them and measure activity against truth, logic, and wisdom. This can occur in conversations after watching movies, hearing news reports, meeting people, and so on.

Principles. Finally, we must offer principles for our kids to live by. These are statements that summarize insights or directives to guide attitudes and actions. It's why we created the Habitudes series for schools and families.[9]

I wish you could meet Gary. He grew up making good grades in school, and consequently, he and his parents visited some prestigious colleges so he could decide which one to attend. He chose Duke University, which pleased Mom and Dad greatly. During a phone conversation his freshmen year, however, Gary grew quiet. Dad could tell something was wrong. When his parents encouraged him to be transparent with them, Gary reluctantly said he didn't like college at all. They were stunned. He was making good grades and was active on campus. What could it be, they wondered. After a moment of awkward silence, Gary finally acknowledged that Duke wasn't the problem. The problem was, he wanted to be an auto mechanic.

This comment seemed completely out of the blue. They knew Gary enjoyed cars but never assumed he wanted to make a career out of them. They assumed he'd be a doctor or an attorney. The more they conversed, however, the more they could tell that repairing cars was Gary's passion.

The good news is, his parents responded perfectly. Gary's dad said, "Then I think we should help you become the best auto mechanic you can possibly be. Why don't you finish out the semester, and let's talk about this goal over the summer."

Together, they decided Gary should attend a technical school to prepare him to run his own garage. Today, he manages a successful auto repair shop and earns a good salary. But more importantly, he's making a difference doing something he loves. Gary found his own fences and passion, and Mom and Dad helped to make it all happen.

Here's to you equipping your kids to construct some great fences of their own.

We Prioritize Being Happy

I have a friend who has two adult children. Her son and daughter are ages 24 and 27. All through their teen years, they seemed to get into trouble as many adolescents do, but my friend, a single mom, never gave up on loving them and forgiving them. It's a divine quality she possesses. She was always good to sit down and discuss why they'd chosen to do what they had done, whether it was to smoke, quit a job, engage in sexual activities, drink at a party, choose poor friends, or even decide whom to marry. I loved the fact that she could talk about anything with her children no matter what the topic was or how old they were. It wasn't until later that I recognized the downside to her parenting style.

When she'd tell me about those conversations, I could tell she was both exhausted and disappointed. She used a phrase over and over that seemed to prevent her from giving the direction her kids desperately needed: "I just want them to be happy."

It's a phrase we've all said regarding what we want for our kids. Who doesn't want their children to be happy? Especially when it comes to the big decisions in their lives, like whom they marry, the career path they choose, where they live, and what they believe about God, life, and values. Our problem is, we parents often don't know how to balance giving wise counsel with our yearning for our teens to be happy.

Today, my friend and both of her adult children are miserable. It's a bit of an irony because happiness was her target. Both kids live at home—one just got fired from a job, and the other just got divorced. One is an alcoholic, and the other is addicted to pornography. Their poor decisions have caught up with them. There is a lot of conversation, but sadly, very little wisdom is being exchanged.

My goal in this chapter is not to suggest our children's happiness is unimportant. My goal is to remind you that happiness should not be a goal. It is a by-product of doing what is right and adding value to others. True satisfaction, for ourselves or our kids, comes from generosity, commitment, and respect for the person in the mirror. The happiest people I know live lives that revolve around serving others, not themselves. In fact, when happiness is the goal instead of a by-product, it is elusive and disappointing. Just ask my friend and her two children.

"Life satisfaction occurs most often when people are engaged in absorbing activities that cause them to forget about themselves, lose track of time and stop worrying," states Claremont Graduate University psychologist Mihaly Csikszentmihalyi. *Flow* is the term Dr. C now uses to describe this state of happiness. People in the flow, young or old, are those who find their strengths (their sweet spot) and serve them up to the world. They lose themselves in the process—and gain happiness. They may be operating on a brain, sewing a dress, solving a problem, or serving in a developing nation, but the flow is what cultivates real satisfaction.[1] It's about adding value to others in the area of our gifts.

Our parenting goal should be to help our kids know how to make wise decisions. Happiness will follow. In fact, fulfillment will follow. Unfortunately, I see so many parents neuter their ability to give valuable guidance to their kids. Instead, they say, "I just want whatever makes them happy." That's about as effective as a shepherd who refuses to guide his sheep because he's afraid he might manipulate them. Remember, happiness is a by-product of wise choices, not a goal to be pursued.

How Parenting Has Changed in the Last Century

Child rearing. Education. Mentoring. Parental psychology. All of these have changed in our lifetime. How did parents in past and foreign cultures train young people to get past themselves and assume adult responsibilities? When you examine past cultures in America, Europe, and Asia, you find a handful of common markers that describe how adults led kids.

- They led by principles. Guiding maxims or beliefs determined their leadership.
- They based their leadership on the belief that there was clearly a right and a wrong behavior.
- They believed that discipline was the first trait a child must learn.
- Their kids routinely interacted with adults in every stage of life.
- They built a desire in their kids' teen years to become adults.
- Their greatest hope was for their children to become adults who contributed to society.

These historic common markers are rare in today's world. The *New Yorker* reports that in a recent study of families in Los Angeles,

> no child routinely performed household chores without being instructed to. Often, the kids had to be begged to attempt the simplest tasks; often, they still refused. In one fairly typical encounter, a father asked his eight-year-old son five times to please go take a bath or a shower. After the fifth plea went unheeded, the father picked the boy up and carried him into the bathroom. A few minutes later, the kid, still unwashed, wandered into another room to play a video game.

> In another encounter, an eight-year-old girl sat down at the dining table. Finding no silverware in front of her, she demanded, "How am I supposed to eat?" The girl clearly knew where the silverware was kept, but her father got up to get it for her.

In a third episode captured on tape, a boy named Ben was supposed to leave the house with his parents. But he couldn't get his feet into his sneakers, because the laces were tied. He handed one of the shoes to his father: "Untie it!" His father suggested that he ask nicely.

"Can you untie it?" Ben replied. After more back-and-forth, his father untied Ben's sneakers. Ben put them on, then asked his father to retie them. "*You* tie your shoes and let's *go*," his father finally exploded. Ben was unfazed. "I'm just *asking*," he said.[2]

What have we done? Why have we changed? Let me suggest a few ideas:

- Now more than ever, we want the approval of our young people. They represent what's cool and hip and relevant. We adults desperately want to be that too.

- We have few or no guiding principles. Many of today's parents were raised when principled living was fading or old-fashioned, so we're just making it up as we go.

- We feel a little messed-up ourselves, so we believe we have no moral authority to ask our kids to do what's right. We'd have to say to them: "Do as I say, not as I do."

- We don't know how to train. We lead toward short-term goals, not long-term ones. We want everyone to be happy now, so we surrender the idea of training kids for the future.

Why Happiness Is Not a Good Goal

We all want happiness, but finding it isn't easy. Many of us think happiness is the end product of material wealth, career goals, and family harmony. With that in mind, we seek the things we believe will deliver it—better cars, nicer houses, and bigger paychecks. Others of us work to put together a large network of friends or find a spouse. When we're not happy with what we have, we believe we'll be happier when we get what we want.

And we're right, we will be happier—for a while. Research reveals, however, that it's a temporary happiness. Whether experiencing a blessing or a tragedy, our happiness levels remain fairly constant in relation to circumstances. Lottery winners and people who have been paralyzed report similar levels of happiness one year after the life-changing event. The initial change from the status quo produces short-term happiness or unhappiness, but as that becomes the day-to-day norm, happiness seems to level out.[3] In fact, people are more prone to go bankrupt after winning the lottery than before. It is an illusion of wealth. Winners who have poor financial habits before winning will eventually return to their prior state. This appears to illustrate that happiness is based on an internal state, not on external circumstances. It is an adjustment we make on the inside, not a goal we pursue on the outside.

--------------------- THE PRINCIPLE ---------------------

When happiness is the goal instead of a by-product,
it is elusive. Life disappoints.

Let's take it a step further with our kids. Studies of twins, both fraternal and identical, indicate that about half of our kids' happiness—or the traits contributing to their happiness, such as an easygoing nature—are genetic.[4] That means half of our kids' ability to be happy has nothing to do with external events, such as careers or lifestyles. That still gives us another half to work with, which means we can control our happiness much more than we might think. Happiness is largely dependent on how we react to or perceive outside events.

I love the story of Todd. When he was in the second grade, his class was not planning to have a Valentine's Day party because they were behind in their schoolwork. Todd told his mother he wanted to exchange valentine cards with friends anyway, even if the school wouldn't throw a party. Because little Todd was a bit of an outcast, his mother knew he may not get cards from his classmates. Fearing that Todd would be disappointed, his mom encouraged him to just prepare a few cards. She quietly wished he would just give up on the idea. But alas, it was not to be. Todd insisted on preparing a card for every single student in his class.

At the end of Valentine's Day, Todd's mother watched him walk up the driveway from the bus stop. As he entered the door, he was talking to himself. "Not one. Not one…" she heard him whisper. Ugh… her worst fears were being realized. Her poor Todd had not received one valentine card.

When she asked him about his day, she braced herself and prepared to comfort him. But little Todd said, "Mom, today was great! I didn't forget one classmate—I gave a card to every one of my friends."

Happiness is all a matter of perspective.

Diagnosing the Emotional Health Problem in Many Kids Today

As I speak to psychologists and career counselors, I've begun to hear a phrase over and over as they describe the emotional state of young people. This phrase appears to be a paradox, but it aptly describes perhaps millions of adolescents in America: "high arrogance, low self-esteem."

How can people be cocky and yet not have a healthy sense of identity? Consider the reality they face. In a recent undergraduate survey, Dr. Art Levine reports that grade inflation has skyrocketed. In 1969, only 7 percent of students said their grade point average was an A- or higher. In 2009, it was 41 percent. In that same time period, students having a C average dropped from 25 percent to 5 percent. But with grade inflation at an all-time high, it's surprising to note that 60 percent of students believe their grades understate the true quality of their work. They believe they deserve a higher mark.[5] One has to wonder— are kids that much smarter than 40 years ago, or do we just give them higher grades to keep the customer? The fact is, student scores continue to decline compared to other nations, but one statistic remains constant—our kids continue to assume they're awesome. So how can they be so dissatisfied?

Parents, teachers, and coaches fear that unhappy kids are a poor reflection on them, so these adults shelter kids and reward them quickly, easily, and repeatedly. Kids naturally begin believing they are amazing. Here's a case in point. My son recently took part in a theater arts competition. Parents paid dearly to enable their kids to get onstage, and now I know why. Every single student got a medal just for showing up. When they performed, they received extra medals. The medal levels were gold, high gold, and platinum. (Did you notice that gold was the lowest award possible?) Here's the clincher—just in case your kid didn't get the award he wanted, trophies were on sale after the competition.

This is not uncommon. Kids today have received trophies for ninth place in Little League baseball. They get fourth runner-up medals at competitions. Ribbons and stars are given out routinely. Of course our kids are arrogant. With little effort at all, they've "earned" a prize.

The problem is, as they age, they begin to suspect this affirmation is skewed. In fact, Mom may be the only one still telling them they're special or amazing. By college, kids meet all kinds of other special and amazing students who are as smart or athletic as they are. Most kids today experience their first real failure between the ages of 17 and 24. When they bump up against hardship and difficulty for the first time in their lives, they often aren't resilient enough to bounce back. They don't know how to handle any degree of failure as young adults.

Truth be told, when kids have heard they are excellent without working hard or truly adding value to a team, the praise rings hollow to them. *Our affirmation must match their performance.* Low self-esteem hits them at this point (often their freshmen or sophomore year in college) because they suddenly recognize their esteem may be built on a foundation of sand. In addition, because many kids are showered with not only affirmation but awards, they can tend to require these prizes to feel good. In short, they need an outward stimulus in order to be happy. In fact, they may feel entitled to rewards because we've told them throughout their lives they're so special.

Raising Emotionally Healthy Kids

My point is not to suggest your child isn't special in his own right. Rather, my point is that this is only part of the story. In preparing our young people for adulthood, we must give them a sense of the big picture. We must mix doses of reality into all the stuff we give them. When I see troubled kids from middle-class homes, I wonder…

- Are they fragile because they've been sheltered?
- Are they unmotivated because they've been praised too quickly?
- Do they get anxious or fearful because they've never taken risks?
- Are they self-absorbed because they've been rewarded so often?
- Do they move back home after college because they're ill-prepared?

I wrestle with this subject in my book *Artificial Maturity: Helping Kids Meet the Challenge of Becoming Authentic Adults*. I suggest that we must communicate two sets of messages to kids (students) during the first two decades of their lives. Sadly, very often only one set of messages gets through. The first ten years, we must communicate childhood messages. If we have done this well, they're prepared for necessary adolescent messages that groom them for a challenging adult world.

Childhood Messages	Adolescent Messages
You are loved.	Life is difficult.
You are unique.	You are not in control.
You have gifts.	You are not that important.
You are safe.	You are going to die.
You are valuable.	Your life is not about you.

I recognize this may sound harsh, but I find myself having to communicate the second set of messages far too often to college students. If we love these kids, we will relay both messages. They deserve the truth from us, and they deserve a childhood that prepares them for the life that awaits them as adults. Will they be emotionally ready to enter adult life? That's up to us.

What Kids Really Need from Adults

Caring adults owe each new generation much more than the gift of happiness. We owe them some perspective. I believe we must be willing to sacrifice their temporary happiness for long-term happiness—including preparing them to be disciplined adults themselves. Instead of pleasure, let's prepare them for fulfillment. What if we borrowed a page from the playbook of the past?

> A few years ago, Izquierdo and Ochs wrote an article for *Ethos*, the journal of the Society of Psychological Anthropology...[They asked,] "Why do Matsigenka children help their families at home more than L.A. children?" And "Why do L.A. adult family members help their children at home more than do Matsigenka?"...
>
> With the exception of the imperial offspring of the Ming dynasty...contemporary American kids may represent the most indulged young people in the history of the world. It's not just that they've been given unprecedented amounts of stuff—clothes, toys, cameras, skis, computers, cell phones, televisions, PlayStations, iPods. (The market for Burberry Baby and other forms of kiddie "couture" has reportedly been growing by 10 percent a year.) They've also been granted unprecedented authority. "Parents want their kids' approval, a reversal of the past ideal of children striving for their parents' approval," Jean Twenge and W. Keith Campbell, both professors of psychology, have written. In many middle-class families, children have one, two, sometimes three adults at their beck and call. This is a social experiment on a grand scale, and a growing number of adults fear that it isn't working out so well: according to one poll, commissioned by *Time* and CNN, two-thirds of American parents think that their children are spoiled.[6]

But who's really to blame? Hmm...we can't just say it's the kids. Let me suggest some key ideas to follow as you lead your young people.

They need to hear the word *watch*.

They need an example from you more than they need entertainment from you. When kids lack direction or discipline, they don't need more diversion. They need an example that demonstrates how to grow wise as they grow up. They need to see adults living for something greater than themselves. They need leaders who show them how to be selfless and sacrificial.

They need to hear the word *practice*.

They need long-term preparation more than short-term happiness. Kids have plenty of amusements that offer pleasure; they need help getting ready for a not-so-pleasurable future, where they'll need to pay their dues on a job for a while. Real satisfaction comes when a person commits to a goal and masters it.

They need to hear the word *no*.

They need a mentor more than a buddy. I decided years ago that my kids have lots of buddies. They have only one dad—that's me. So I must play the card that isn't always fun but that earns their future love and respect. This means they may not like me each week of their childhood or adolescence. If I earn their respect through leading them well, love will eventually and naturally follow.

They need to hear the word *wait*.

Today, most things happen quickly with little wait time. Our ability to delay gratification has shrunk. Parents, teachers, coaches, employers, and youth pastors need to build wait time into the game plan for their young people as a rehearsal for adult life. Kids naturally become happy when they learn to appreciate waiting for something they want and delaying gratification.

They need to hear the word *serve*.

Unlike other cultures in history, we've made the pursuit of happiness a part of our American tradition. It's in the Declaration of

Independence because service was so imbedded into the society at the time. Being happy was a relatively new thought to that generation. Today, we breed consumers more than we do contributors—producing dissatisfied kids. All I can say is, it's no wonder.

I was taken back when I read a recent headline: "Massachusetts principal calls off Honors Night because it could be 'devastating' to students who missed the mark."

> A Massachusetts principal has been criticized for cancelling his school's Honors Night, saying it could be "devastating" to the students who worked hard, but fell short of the grades.
>
> [The principal] notified parents last week of his plan to eliminate the event.
>
> "The Honors Night, which can be a great source of pride for the recipients' families, can also be devastating to a child who has worked extremely hard in a difficult class but who, despite growth, has not been able to maintain a high grade point average," [he] penned in his first letter to parents.[7]

That appears to be the goal today in so many schools—to make sure we don't hurt anyone's feelings. We want all kids to be happy and feel as though life is fair.

I get this. The problem is, it's not a good long-term decision.

Think about the long-term consequences of this decision. First, these young teens now begin to expect life to be fair—if we all can't get awards, then no one does. That's just not how life works, and it's certainly not how employment works. Second, it removes their need to cope with loss. No one was recognized as excellent, so no one learned to handle not getting the spotlight. Sadly, this is not even remotely similar to the world they're about to enter as adults.

We must help our kids see the big picture. There's always another side to the coin. Just ask Cristian Mojica.

Cristian is a high school student at Boston Latin Academy. He is a football player and swimmer who was far more serious about sports than his academic development—until this year.

What did it take?

Sitting on the side of the pool with a stopwatch, timing other swimmers.

His coach, who happens to be his dad, decided his son needed to change and see the bigger picture. Mojica had a 1.66 grade point average last winter, and athletes are required to have a 1.67 GPA to participate.

"I honestly don't think he took it that serious last year and he didn't think it was a big deal and he'd be able to slide by. Well guess what, he didn't," his dad said. "He came to me and said 'What can you do?' I said 'Cristian, there's nothing I can do.' He needed to learn a lesson."

So the teen studied and clocked the other swimmers for weeks. The result?

The junior later got to compete in the swimming city championships, *and* he was named the Boston Scholar Athletes' February Scholar-Athlete of the Month with a 3.2 grade point average. Not bad.

"At the beginning of my high school career, I never would have thought I would be nominated for that because my grades weren't where they should have been," Mojica said during a recent swim meet. "But now I stepped my grades up so it feels good to be nominated."[8]

His dad knew it was in him all the time—and simply seized the moment.

Years ago, my wife helped to start a community theater program. Students between the ages of 8 and 18 could take drama classes and audition for shows each year. It provided a great outlet for hundreds of kids who weren't athletes but had gifts in other areas.

Because my wife cofounded the program, she spoke to our kids about what life would look like if they got involved. There would be no special favors, they would not automatically get a part in the shows, and Mom could not join the panel of judges when they auditioned. She made sure no parent assumed our kids would get extra perks. In fact, quite the opposite—we probably went overboard making sure our kids didn't feel entitled to anything extraordinary.

In the end, this enabled our kids to mature. With no entitlements or favors, they found satisfaction in looking outward, seeing the big picture, and making sure others were recognized. Ironically, I believe the no-perks situation actually helped our kids become happier people.

My son's fifth-grade year was a tough one. His best friend moved away, leaving him without a classmate who shared his interests. He wasn't gifted at sports, so recess became a lonely time for him. He never complained, but my wife and I could tell he was miserable. Our normally fun-loving son grew quiet and reserved. He moved from social to withdrawn in a matter of weeks. When we finally asked him what he did on the playground, he replied, "Oh, I just walk around by myself." I cringed, but when I began trying to "fix" the problem, my son added, "It's okay, Dad. Recess gives me lots of time to think."

Needless to say, I was proud of the fact that Jonathan never once whined or expected us to fix things. Together, we sought a solution that enabled him to get beyond his misery. Things turned around when he got involved with the community theater program. In it, he encountered an entirely new circle of friends and was able to use his gifts in a meaningful way. The answer did not lie in him chasing his own happiness, but in him discovering a place where he could see and serve beyond himself.

Just to be clear, I love my two kids and want them to be happy for a lifetime. And because I do, I taught them not to settle for pursuing happiness as a selfish pleasure. Life is quite a paradox. If happiness is the goal for our kids, we will create consumers who want and need more and more in order to make them happy. But if giving rather than receiving is the goal, happiness is almost always the result.

We Are Inconsistent

When our children were ages four and eight, I noticed symptoms in them that troubled me. Both our daughter and son were acting out a bit too much. They were rebelling and pushing the boundaries we had clearly set. I recognized these were normal temptations for many children's temperaments, but it wasn't typical behavior for our kids. My wife and I began talking about what we were observing. Our kids were...

- talking back when given clear and simple instructions
- experiencing insecurities about trips we'd take to new places
- displaying bad attitudes about their food or daily chores
- refusing to obey immediately when asked to do something

At first these seemed like random, unrelated challenges. But then we acknowledged something we were doing as parents. We had hit a busy season of our lives and were inadvertently playing defense rather than offense in our parenting. We were exhausted at the end of each day, and frankly, some nights were about survival rather than good parenting. We'd lay down a rule and then change it when it was broken and we didn't have time to enforce it. For example, we might tell our daughter to be in bed by eight p.m., but when a TV show came on at that time, she'd lobby to watch it...and we'd eventually give in. I think this is fine once in a while on special occasions, but our caving began to be the rule instead of an exception.

Our inconsistencies weren't huge, but as we racked up several of them, they began to breed negative attitudes and behaviors in our kids. They learned that if they argued long enough, they could wear us down and eventually get their way. As our parental leadership vacillated, our kids felt uncertain about their boundaries. In short, a lot of little uncertainties produced a few big insecurities. Our parental inconsistency resulted in our kids' insecurity. Parenting experts and psychologists Jesse Rutherford and Kathleen Nickerson write about this.

> No matter how well you've selected your rules, how much you praise your kids, or how effectively you discipline them, you must be consistent, or your efforts will be in vain and your household will still be in crisis. Kids need consistency to get the message because your actions speak louder than your words—it's part of how they're wired.[1]

THE PRINCIPLE
When we are inconsistent, we send mixed signals and breed insecurity and instability in our kids.

My wife and I learned something we all know deep in our intuition. When parents give in to our children's requests and demands, we send them mixed signals. At first, they like it. After all, they just won the argument. They got what they wanted. In time, however, our constant *caving* begins to foster a constant *craving* in them. They want clarity. With boundaries unclear, they need more direct attention from Mom or Dad. Unwittingly, we actually breed insecurity and instability in our kids.

This may sound strange, but consistency may be your best friend as a parent because it aids in your authority and in your child's development.

Over the past decade, neuroscientists have reached milestones in brain research. We know more than ever about how our brains grow and function. One discovery is plain and simple—brain cells grow when they are stimulated. They are strengthened and expanded with consistent use, just as any other muscles are. When we practice doing something, we get better because our brain adapts to that function. Conscious conduct becomes subconscious. Habits form. Grooves are laid. This is especially true in childhood, when the brain is forming faster than during adulthood. This is why learning a new language is easier for children than for adults.

This is also why consistency is most important during childhood. Tracks are laid that our kids may follow for years to come—maybe for a lifetime. Actions that happen consistently have a better chance of becoming permanent. It's the old adage—practice doesn't make perfect, it makes permanent. So think for a moment about what's most consistent in your home right now. Is it...

arguing   meals apart

discipline   meals together

poor communication   addictions to screens

great communication   love

Dr. Nickerson continues:

> Sticking with a new endeavor is what makes it become a habit, and the sooner you start, the easier it will be for both you and your child. What's going on around your child strongly impacts the development of his brain. In order for your child's brain cells to learn the new rewards, rules, and consequences, and to behave accordingly in a way that becomes automatic, you must remain consistent while his brain develops.[2]

The Benefits of Consistency

Emotionally speaking, consistency makes kids feel safe. When they know what to expect, they feel secure. When their relationship with you, the caring adult, is consistent and solid, they feel more stable. Clear boundaries, steady consequences, reliable rewards, and the assurance that they can count on you like a sunrise each morning… these things provide the security, safety, and stability your children need. And only then can they reach their maximum potential as students, employees, and future spouses and parents. When discipline is consistent, it unlocks all kinds of barriers and solves all sorts of problems. In fact, I'd go so far as to say choosing between strict or lenient rules isn't as important as being consistent in applying them both at home and in public.

You may need to remove your child from a restaurant or a store to consistently execute a rule, but it's worth it. Repetition is a teacher, and execution is the principal. The follow-through is what actually seals the deal and changes behavior.

I'll never forget hearing about a mother who kept losing battles over the rules with Bradley, her eight-year-old son—especially in public. Whenever she warned him that she'd punish him for breaking a rule, Bradley would threaten to take off his clothes right there in a department store or some other public place. One day they were in a toy store buying a birthday gift for his friend, and Bradley demanded his mother buy him a toy. When she refused, he threatened to take his clothes off. She stayed steady for a moment, but the boy began unbuttoning his shirt. She caved, and he won. Sadly, this was a pattern. Over time, Bradley became more volatile as Mom's only consistency was in her wavering.

Bradley finally met his match at the dentist's office. He hopped onto the chair while his mother stood nearby. The dentist requested she step out of the room and relax in the waiting room. She obliged. At this point, the dentist asked Bradley to open his mouth for the cleaning. Bradley refused, saying he didn't want to. The dentist replied that Bradley needed his teeth cleaned and that he would wait as long as it took. At that point, Bradley threatened to take off his clothes. The dentist sat down and said, "Go ahead, son."

The defiant boy slowly unfastened a few buttons of his shirt, waiting for the dentist to stop him. The dentist waited patiently. Bradley warned him he really would take all his clothes off, but the dentist remained calm, saying he was okay with that. The boy continued slowly, removing his socks, shirt, and pants…down to his underwear. The dentist then asked, "Is this really what you want to do?" At this point, he gathered Bradley's clothes from the floor, took him firmly by the hand, and led him out into a waiting room that was filled with patients. The boy stood in his underwear as the dentist handed the clothes to his mother. The dentist simply said, "Let's try another day when Bradley is willing to cooperate with me." And he sent them home. Mom left with a little more resolve, and Bradley with a little more humility. That was the last time that kid ever threatened to disrobe again—but it took an adult who followed through.

When adults are consistent with rules, rewards, and consequences, kids begin to think, "Okay, I understand what to expect. I may not like the rules, but I know they are real, I'm not being singled out, and there will be consequences for not following them." When we are consistent, most kids choose to stay within the boundaries, which we set up for their welfare anyway. Consistency fosters happy and contented kids. On the other hand, without it, children feel their world is in flux, and they may become anxious and more defiant. In this state, you can expect them to test the rules much more to see if you really mean what you say. This can exhaust a parent or teacher quickly. Consistency actually makes your life easier.

Consistency with Teens

"Did you not hear me? I told you seven times to clean up your room! What is wrong with you?" This scenario between parents and teens happens millions of times every year. In this new phase of life, adolescents sometimes act as if their listening skills shrink and their emotions expand. Does this sound familiar?

It's very common for adolescents to push the envelope. It's natural for them to test boundaries because they're wired to spread their wings and become individuals as they move from childhood to adulthood. This is normal in their maturation process. If they enter puberty without consistent leadership, this period of their life becomes even more difficult. They are already feeling uneasy about their identity—their hormones are changing, their brain is developing in new ways, and peer pressure is reaching an all-time high. It's common for teens to fail to listen to parents, especially if their parents are inconsistent in following through on what they've said.

Think about it. When we waver back and forth on our word, we actually foster their inclination to ignore our imperatives. Why should they listen? We will likely change our minds. In fact, as adults we don't even listen to or respect those who say one thing and do another. Why would we expect anything else from a teenager?

Another symptom of our inconsistency shows up when our teens react to our hollow statements or overstatements. They don't respond well when we threaten to do something we have no intention of actually doing. In the emotion of the moment, we exaggerate and say things that we don't really mean.

- I'm grounding you for the rest of the year!
- Unless you come in right now, I'm going to break both your legs.
- If your grades don't improve, I'm sending you to boarding school.
- If you don't stop that, you can't talk on your cell phone all summer.
- If you don't quiet down, I'm gonna kill you!

Surely you've heard other similar statements from parents. Our teenagers know we have no intention to follow through on those exaggerated threats. In fact, we're saying, "Don't listen to me because I say things I really don't mean. Just stand your ground and argue. I'll eventually cave." Bottom line, using threats like these is futile because we lose credibility and our children continue the very behavior we are trying to change. Even good kids harass and nag their parents—it's part of growing up! But the parents are responsible to avoid creating a volatile environment. When parents consistently follow through on their word, they reduce the number of emotional firestorms that erupt with their teenagers.

Failing to Hold Them Accountable

We are also inconsistent when we tell our children to do something but don't check to see that it's been done. Does this sound familiar? You tell your daughter she can't leave the house until she cleans her room. She enters her room while you're busy doing laundry. In a few minutes she says, "I'm leaving." When you ask, "Did you clean your room?" she says yes and leaves. Half an hour later you happen to pass her room and notice that she didn't pick up a thing.

Not every child or teenager needs strict accountability, but most do. It is in our human nature—our sinful nature—to push boundaries and test limits. It's what nudges kids to lie, cheat, or even steal. Some children try to get away with as much as they possibly can. If we fail to be consistent, if we don't hold them accountable to do what we've requested or what they've agreed to do, we harm their development. We can actually condition kids to be manipulative.

Depending on the mood we're in or how our day has gone, we may treat the same behavior in different ways. For instance, one morning our kid may be rude, and we react by giving him a lecture. Later, when that same rudeness occurs, we may ignore it. Or the following day when our firstborn child behaves a certain way, we put her on restriction. But when our "baby" acts the same way, he often gets by with privileges our firstborn never knew. At some point, this will become an elephant in the room. The oldest child is going to bring it up one day. Get ready to explain.

Instead of reacting inconsistently, try setting up a standard equation. Whenever your kids act up or talk back in a certain way, they will lose some phone privileges or have a new curfew time. Setting up equations and consequences for all will reduce inconsistency and make the environment more calm and predictable. Jayne Rutherford and Kathleen Nickerson call this "interpersonal consistency." It's all about creating a predictable response for kids. These equations can help children, young or old, feel more secure because you've established codes right up front, such as a set amount of time for...

talking on the phone each night
being online each day
watching television
socializing with friends
having dinner together

Why Are We Inconsistent?

Let me suggest some common reasons why we parents may find consistency difficult. Perhaps this list can serve to spark changes in your family.

We lack a compass to make decisions.

Perhaps the number one reason we aren't consistent is that we lack courage. And often, we lack courage because we aren't sure what should be done. It's true in almost any situation—at work, at school, in our community, and certainly at home with our children.

We are family friends with a single mom named Darla and her daughter, Stacy. We love them deeply, which makes some of our conversations difficult. Stacy, a minor, is dating Heath, who is over 21. He doesn't seem to understand the ramifications of dating an underage female. Issues like alcohol and curfew and sexual boundaries are all huge for both Darla and Stacy, but Heath continues to push for more autonomy. Both Stacy and Darla are torn over how to handle the situation.

(Quite frankly, single moms are my heroes. They may just have the toughest job in the world—being the breadwinner, parent, coach, and disciplinarian for their children.)

Darla has struggled being the "bad cop" and often finds herself giving in to Heath and Stacy's requests because she's tired of squabbling *and* because she's unsure about what to enforce in today's culture. She doesn't want to be old-fashioned, but she doesn't feel comfortable with some of the things Heath and Stacy want to do. I suggest her chief problem is she doesn't have a clear family moral compass. When we talked about drawing some lines in the sand to clarify what she would permit and what she wouldn't, life became easier for all of them. Heath eventually got used to the compass and is cooperating.

As a parent or leader, if I am fuzzy on what should happen next, I tend to be fuzzy in my direction and in my behavior. I may waver back and forth, trying to figure out my dilemma as I go. It's like building a bridge as you cross it. It's very difficult.

We've grown accustomed to delegating to professionals.

Our nation was thrust into the "service economy" when the first batch of Baby Boomers became adults in the 1960s. We now pay for professionals to serve us in ways our grandparents never did—to change the oil in our cars, to serve us food, to clean our clothes, to care for our lawn, to fix things around the house...you name it. I actually believe it's changed the way we raise our kids. How often have we outsourced our top priority—to set an example for our children or help them make good decisions? Why do we expect a professional—a stranger!—to do our parental job for us? It brings us back to the issue of being inconsistent. Sometimes we want to be in control and lead our children to face a bright future. Then hours later, we are exhausted and want someone else to take our kids for us and help fashion them into the adults they should be. In today's culture, counselors and church youth groups are forced to take on responsibilities that parents in former times never delegated.

Let's face it. Sometimes we're on an emotional roller coaster. The demands on our lives are so great today—the complexity of our involvements and the cost for the lifestyle we want—they can wear us down. It's no wonder we become inconsistent. On good days, we are the best parents in the world, loving and wise, kind and forgiving. On our bad days, however, we can turn from Dr. Jekyll to Mr. Hyde. That's when we try to temporarily delegate the parenting task to some other gifted person—a soccer coach, a teacher, a youth pastor, a counselor, or an uncle or aunt. The job of navigating tough times with our kids is laborious; it's not meant for the fainthearted.

I appreciate the input of other adults in our children's lives, but I can never delegate or farm out this top priority in my life.

We are not on the same page.

You and your spouse are not likely to be consistent if you're not on the same page. Consistency must come from both mother and father as a unit. Both parents must mean what they say when dealing with a child, and they must support one another.

Recently, Jesse asked his mom, "Can I go to a concert tonight?" She replied no. He then asked his father the same question and got a yes. When concert time came, Jesse started getting dressed to go. His mother saw him and asked what he was doing. He responded that he was going to the concert because Dad said he could. Mom confronted Dad, which started an argument. In the meantime, Jesse finished getting dressed and left for the concert.

This inconsistency sabotages parental authority. It undermines each parent's word and forces them to focus on the division between them rather than the child's request. Bingo—that's exactly what Jesse wanted. The kid learns to manipulate, playing one parent against the other. One parent's authority is diminished. The other parent has contradicted the other, forcing a showdown. In addition, this approach tends to identify one parent as the bad cop and the other as the good cop, which almost always harms parental connection and fosters fights. Caregivers (including parents, aunts, uncles, grandparents) must work as a unit. If you disagree with each other, demonstrate a united front to your children and resolve to discuss your differences later in private.

We are busy with the demands of work on top of family.

This excerpt of an article from the United Kingdom shows that this problem isn't unique to the United States.

> Growing number of mothers and fathers are expecting schools to teach their children the difference between right and wrong, acceptable levels of behaviour and social norms, it is claimed.
>
> Richard Watson, a futurologist and founder of What's Next, which charts trends in society…said schools were

increasingly expected to teach beyond conventional subjects to give children a moral framework for their lives.

It has resulted in parents blaming teachers—and threatening legal action—if their children subsequently go off the rails or misbehave outside the classroom.

"One of the things I am fascinated by is the extent to which parents outsource the moral education and guidance of their children because they are too busy to do it themselves," he said.

"You get very busy parents—usually both of them working—who effectively drop the kids off at school at the age of five and pick them up when they are 18 years old, and they want the school to do absolutely everything.

"It is not just about the day-to-day stuff and making sure they do their homework, it's the entire moral education of that child.

"Parents can't do that. If they expect their children to turn out as well balanced individuals, they have got to be involved as well."[3]

Learning Consistency from Surprising Places

Like many parents, [David and Eleanor Starr] were trapped between the smooth-running household they aspired to have and the exhausting, earsplitting one they actually lived in. "I was trying the whole 'love them and everything will work out' philosophy," Eleanor said, "but it wasn't working."[4]

So what did they do? They decided to borrow a page from the playbook for corporate America. They began to run their family like a business. Yes, you read that right. A business. By this, I don't mean things became cold and calloused, nor did anyone get fired from the family if they underperformed. But David began to organize chores, weekly meetings, and accountability—just like thousands of companies across the United States. It has worked brilliantly.

> They turned to a cutting-edge program called Agile Development that has rapidly spread from manufacturers in Japan to startups in Silicon Valley. It's a system of group dynamics in which workers are organized into small teams, hold daily progress sessions and weekly reviews. Accountability is key. As David explained, "Having weekly family meetings increased communication, improved productivity, lowered stress, and made everyone much happier to be part of the family team"…
>
> A new generation of parents is now taking solutions from the workplace and transferring them to the home. From accountability checklists to family branding sessions, from time-shifting meals to more efficient conflict resolution, families are finally reaping the benefits of decades of groundbreaking research into group dynamics. The result is a bold new blueprint for happy families.
>
> Surveys show that both parents and children list stress as their No. 1 concern. A chief source of that stress is change. Just as kids stop teething, they start throwing tantrums; just as they stop needing us to give them a bath, they need our help dealing with online hazing. No wonder psychologist Salvador Minuchin said that the most important characteristic of families is being "rapidly adaptable."[5]

It seems to me that systems like this—complete with 20-minute family meetings—could provide peace to a chaotic home. And the key to it all is accountability and consistency.

Four Debts We Owe Our Children

For years, our nation has experienced an economic downturn. The national debt is embarrassing, and the value of the US dollar is lower than it's been in years. Our kids will be paying off our debts all their lives.

Greater than this debt, however, is a debt I believe adults owe the next generation. It's a debt that has more to do with our character than our cash. When I see troubled young people, I can usually trace their struggles back to poor leadership they received growing up. I believe adults must rethink the way we lead our kids. Whether we are parents, teachers, coaches, employers, or youth workers, we owe four debts to our kids today.

Clarity fosters focused direction.

Clarity is one of the greatest gifts adults can give children. In fact, it is one of the rarest gifts leaders provide their teams. In this day of uncertainty, we must furnish clear values and a clear role model for what healthy adults look like. Clarity fosters focused direction. It promotes ambition instead of ambiguity. As much as possible, consider how to avoid being fuzzy about morals or ethics and about the right step of action in circumstances. Remember—you are not raising kids, you are raising future adults.

Where do you need to be more clear as you lead your kids?

Transparency fosters validation and vulnerability.

Transparency is contagious. When leaders model it, becoming candid about their own flaws and failures, they cultivate the same level of honesty in those who follow. Young people are not likely to disclose their own struggles unless they believe they're in a safe environment to do so. When adults model transparency, they validate the young people who are listening. The kids realize they're not alone. Transparency also invites honesty and vulnerability on their part.

Where do you need to be more transparent as you lead your kids?

Boundaries foster security.

The word *boundary* is typically perceived as negative. Boundaries hem people in and keep others out. They're dividing lines. Yet boundaries are precisely what youth need as they figure out who they are. Just as a train needs tracks in order to make progress, so it is with students. The tracks kids run on must be furnished by adults at first. Boundaries don't prevent growth and progress, they actually encourage it. When kids receive the boundaries, they gain a deep sense of security and safety. Boundaries keep their exploration from being destructive.

Where do you need to provide better boundaries as you lead your kids?

Consistency fosters trust and assurance.

As I reflect on my own parents, the greatest gift they gave me (apart from love) was consistency of leadership and values. Parents often ask me how strict they should be with their kids. I think how strict we are is less important than how consistent we are once we set the boundaries. Consistency in our leadership with kids fosters trust and assurance in them. They know what they can count on. They can begin to take more risks and even extend themselves with their time and energy because they know they are safe.

Where do you need to be more consistent as you lead your kids?

Last year, I read an inspiring story about Dawn Loggins. At the time, Dawn was a high school senior in Lawndale, North Carolina. She grew up in a ramshackle home with no electricity or running water. She often went weeks without showering. Dawn was eventually abandoned by her drug-abusing parents—she came home one day, and they were gone. Dawn was suddenly a homeless teenager.

She made a decision very rapidly. She didn't want the lifestyle her parents had modeled for her—a volatile life of ups and downs, living hand to mouth. So she began sleeping at friends' homes and got a job as a janitor at her high school. She showed up early to mop floors, clean restrooms, and wipe down chalkboards…all the while reviewing for tests in that classroom herself.

The head custodian noticed something different about Dawn's lifestyle and soon discovered she had no home. The custodian offered

Dawn a place to stay indefinitely. Soon, teachers and others in town pitched in, donating clothes and providing medical and dental care.

Driven by a life she did not want, Dawn soon was modeling the consistent life she wished her parents had known. She said she feels sorry for them, but the whole episode has ignited her ambition to make something of herself. She not only works before and after school but also studies hard and makes straight As. Dawn recently applied to Harvard University and was accepted. Amazing. This girl will go from homeless to Harvard.

Dawn doesn't claim to be anyone special. But she is a vivid example of a kid whose potential was unleashed when she moved from inconsistency to consistency.

We Remove the Consequences

Matt is a 29-year-old employee who was let go from his job. He plans to sue his employer for being treated unfairly. When I heard his story, I probed a bit deeper and instantly recognized he had no case. The unfair treatment he received was due to the fact that his supervisor didn't allow him to be on Facebook during work hours. In addition, Matt claimed his boss expected him to log a minimum number of sales calls each day. Sadly, he was failing to do so. Finally, he claimed his supervisor threatened to let him go if he continued to arrive at work late. He'd done so three days in one week, but he contends it was due to bad traffic. Who can control bad traffic? The young man blamed his company for his misfortune, but I know otherwise. Plenty of younger and less talented team members were showing up on time and flourishing on the same job. This man's problem was he never owned his behavior. He was completely irresponsible, even as a grown man.

How could this happen, you ask? I bet you can guess.

Let me begin by saying he was conditioned to be irresponsible for all of his 29 years. His mother was always bailing him out of trouble. She actually joined him for the job interview. He simply learned to lean on her for anything and everything he needed—from taking his backpack to school when he forgot it as a child to paying for his speeding tickets in high school. She was Superman and he was Lois Lane. Trouble was, he was always in trouble, needing someone to come to his aid. Ultimately, he was disabled.

This problem is not limited to grown men.

I stood in front of an audience of parents, talking about how to help our children make progress and prevent them from sabotaging themselves along the way. Once this issue popped up in the question and answer session, the room was buzzing with opinions. Unfortunately, no one seemed to embrace a long-term solution.

One mother reported that her young son threw a fit every time his soccer team lost. He went ballistic—screaming, throwing things, and even getting violent if someone tried to stop him. The mom's solution? For as long as possible, she would simply tell her little boy the game ended in a tie.

Another parent shared how his daughter struggled with lying to her teacher, her friends, and her mom and dad. It was chronic dishonesty. Over the years, her father appeased everyone by covering for her, explaining that she battled with low self-esteem and would often lie or exaggerate to feel as if she were measuring up. Her dad would make as many phone calls as it took to defend his tenth-grade daughter until he had appeased the offended party. Unfortunately, the parent revealed that his little girl was now unable to get a job as a teen because nobody trusted her.

That evening, one story after another arose from the crowd, each one a tale of a dad or mom who knew no other way to demonstrate love for their children than to cover for them, give in to them, lie for them, excuse their conduct, or negotiate for them. In the short run, none of their coping mechanisms were horrific. In the long run, however, they created all kinds of problems for both the parents and the children. When we insulate kids and remove consequences from actions, we fail to prepare them for the future that awaits them as they mature.

An Art and a Science

Parenting is both an art and a science. Few of us received any training for it. Americans average 12 to 14 years of school before they enter their careers. We go through classes, study, and take a test to get a license to drive a car. Yet we are thrust into the parenting journey with no such preparation. Most of us begin molding the life of an emerging adult without ever reading a book on the subject. One of the most common mistakes we make (for lack of training) is the one we'll discuss in this chapter. We want our kids to be happy, content, and well-adjusted. When conflict arises, our first inclination is to solve the problem for them. After all, we are their leaders.

Removing the consequences takes one of two roads. We either excuse their behavior and remove negative outcomes, or we actually step in and pay the consequence for them.

When we do this, we frequently relieve the stress. We bring immediate peace to the situation, so we get addicted to this pattern. Unfortunately, we don't see the long-term problems we are causing. Removing the consequences from our children's lives brings short-term tranquility but long-term trouble.

THE PRINCIPLE

When we insulate kids and remove
consequences from actions, we fail to prepare them
for the future that awaits them.

Why Do We Remove Consequences?

We don't want them to suffer.

This is likely the top reason we swoop in and come to their aid or make excuses for their poor conduct. We don't want our children to undergo any pain. Only a sadistic parent would, right? The problem is, if we really believe this, we contradict ourselves because the consequences our kids will experience as adults will be more severe than the consequences they experience as kids. By removing consequences for our children now, we just postpone and increase their pain. We are wise to allow a child-sized dose of suffering now to avoid much greater pain in their lives later. Parents must learn to empathize with their child's future self—their adult self.

We want to prevent any disadvantages.

We're convinced our kids are going somewhere. We undo mistakes they make because we don't want them to fall behind in any way. Often, we do this because we are living out our unlived lives through our children. This is when we must understand the difference between sympathy and empowerment. Our kids don't need us to solve their problems for them out of sympathy. They need us to empower them to solve their own problems.

It's easier.

If we're honest, part of the reason we remove consequences for our kids is that it's easier than facing the emotional trauma of watching them suffer consequences. Our kids can wear us down. They may throw a tantrum, give us the silent treatment, become extremely emotional, or any number of reactions to negative outcomes. It is easier to raise the white flag, surrender, and just solve the problem ourselves.

We want them to have great self-esteem.

Sometimes we remove consequences because we feel negative situations will harm kids' self-esteem. This can indeed happen in an insecure family, but these difficult circumstances can actually promote their self-esteem—if we'll empower them to go through obstacles and adversities well. Talking through the situation and encouraging them to follow through to the end can be the best self-esteem boosters imaginable.

We want to get our children to love us.

Many parents feel it's important that their children love them. They make it their purpose to elicit their child's love as they interact. This is damaging. The purpose of our parenting is to prepare our children for life so they can eventually leave the nest ready and strong enough to fend for themselves. If we really love our kids, we do not make it our aim to get them to love us back. That is the by-product of our loving them and leading them into adulthood. Our kids don't need us to be their pals—they need us to be their parents.

We want to be in control.

Much of our problem, as parents, is the result of our pursuit of control. We are the most controlling population of parents in recent history. We feel as if our public schools aren't doing a good enough job, the local soccer team doesn't give our kid enough playing time, the theater arts program didn't cast our daughter with enough lines in the play…and we feel we must step in and control the situation. But we must recognize that control is a myth. We are not in control. Life is bigger than us, and the sooner we equip our kids to handle the ups and downs of it, the better off they are.

Is This About Now or Later?

Perhaps this is the biggest adjustment we must make—to stop pursuing control. To learn to trust and to empower our kids to navigate their way through life without the misconception that they can control it. *Adaptability* should be our aim, not control.

The fact is, we often live, lead, and parent only for today. We just want peace right now, and we forget the long-term impact on our kids. My mother and father modeled long-term parenting all through my growing-up years. When I stole something as a young kid, I had to march down to the store and give it back with an apology. If I lied or cheated, it was the same thing. Consequences came even if it was a little white lie or cheating on a very small problem. Why? It was the principle of the thing. My parents knew I was forming long-term patterns in my life every day. I learned a huge axiom over the years: The further out I can see, the better decision I make as a parent. Author Hara Estroff-Marano emphasizes the importance of allowing kids to struggle.

> Research demonstrates that children who are protected from grappling with difficult tasks don't develop what psychologists call "mastery experiences." Kids who have this well-earned sense of mastery are more optimistic and decisive; they've learned they are capable of overcoming adversity and achieving goals.[1]

Kids who've never tested their abilities grow into emotionally brittle young adults who are more vulnerable to anxiety and depression.

According to one US poll, the majority of parents admit their kids have too little responsibility. Compared to their parents' generation or grandparents' generation, we've busied our children with soccer games and piano recitals but not with real responsibility such as work, service, or even chores around the house. A kid can learn some disciplines from games or recitals, but authentic responsibility comes from the real world, where we serve others who cannot help themselves or in exchange for a paycheck. The exchange has an internal effect on us, even as kids. Why? Because the consequences are real. Losing isn't simply about a soccer scoreboard or messing up on a song in a recital, but about affecting real people. As our kids grow older, the benefits and the consequences must become real.

What Happens If We Fail to Do This?

If adults fail to learn this important truth, what kind of adults will our kids grow up to be?

- *Irresponsible.* They won't have ownership of their life; they'll learn to blame others.
- *Lazy.* They will have a poor work ethic and perhaps low creativity levels.
- *Dependent.* They won't be self-sufficient; they'll be unready for autonomy.
- *Emotionally brittle.* They will have few coping skills and won't develop resilience.

Are We Stealing Ambition from Our Kids?

Recently, after visiting family friends, I learned their son Jacob had won another trophy on his Little League baseball team. When he invited me to see it, I noticed it was in a room full of trophies. I assumed his team had won several championships, but alas, I was wrong. Jacob had never won a championship.

I soon discovered that every one of his awards was simply for playing on a team.

Some social scientists actually call this generation Trophy Kids. We are raising a generation of kids who are used to receiving recognition for participating, not for winning. It started back in the 1980s when moms and dads were determined to boost their kids' self-esteem and encourage participation more than conquest. I understand that—I am one of those parents. But I believe this works when children are five, not when they're ten or eleven. It has backfired, and we're now reaping the consequences of this decision. I know a kid who gave a trophy back to his dad after an awards ceremony and said, "This doesn't mean anything." These kids are not stupid. Are we?

What Were We Thinking?

Reflect for a moment on the long-term impact of this kind of world. When coaches let children swing at a ball until they hit it (there are no strikeouts), when they decide not to keep score (there are no losers), and when everyone gets an equal award in the end (we are all equal), we take away the kids' motivation—especially the boys'. We take the steam out of their engine. They begin to think, "Why try? I'm going to get the same reward whether I put out any effort or not." And it's easier to put out no effort.

This is not just about sports either. We so wanted these kids to feel special, we began to take away the possibility of failing a class. Students always seem to find a way to negotiate a grade or do some extra credit work to make up for failing to do what they'd been asked to do. Many parents have removed the possibility of failing at home. Kids receive money or perks even if they fail to share the responsibilities around the house. As a result, college staff and faculty report that incoming students are making comments like these:

- Why didn't I get an A? I showed up to class every day.

- You're guaranteeing me a job once I graduate, right?

- OK...so I flunked the test. What do I need to do to get the grade I want?

- How come my roommate got a scholarship and I didn't?

- If my parents pay the tuition, I deserve the grades I want.

- I think the government's job is to make sure I get a job and a house.
- You can't criticize me. I tried.

I mentioned in chapter 2 that three classes of young students were asked to draw pictures. The first group was told, "When you're finished, you will get a prize." The second group wasn't told anything about prizes, but each student got one after they drew the picture. The third group was told nothing about prizes and received no prizes when finished. The result? When given the opportunity to draw a second picture—with no rewards or prizes—not one student in the first group of kids wanted to draw anything. Most kids in the second class and all the kids in the third class participated and drew a second picture. Why? Their motivation wasn't a reward in the first place.

Hmm…the motivation for the first group was reduced to an outward reward. The third group drew pictures for the sheer intrinsic reward of creating art. The lesson? In our effort to praise or reward students, we have stolen the satisfaction of the work itself. In giving them something for nothing, we're stealing ambition from them.

By wanting our children and students to be happy, we may have created the most depressed population of kids in recent history. By leading them in this way, we have all but removed the ambition in them. We have most certainly diminished it. Here's the reason why this philosophy has holes in it.

As their possibility of failure goes down, so does their value of success.

Think about it. If I grow up in a world where almost everything has been given to me or made easy, I start feeling entitled to it. In fact, I stop trying hard because I know that an adult will ensure I get what I need or want.

One of the most valuable commodities we can cultivate in this emerging generation is ambition. By this I don't mean selfish ambition or self-absorbed preoccupation. (Narcissism may or may not motivate a kid to try.) I am speaking of the internal drive to achieve and to grow. The motivation to excel in an area. The satisfaction of applying gifts and talents to something more than a video game. This internal motivation comes from struggling and achieving—and also from serving or adding value to others.

We feel most valuable when we add value to other people.

We can't conjure up self-esteem in kids by giving them a few affirming statements or a ribbon for being pretty or showing up on time. Kids develop self-esteem when they know who they are intrinsically and use their gifts to contribute to a cause greater than themselves. I firmly believe ambition is part of the equation. Ambition builds self-esteem and vice versa. When I feel good about myself, I tend to try harder. And when I try harder, I tend to feel better about myself.

So What Can We Do?
Let them struggle, and if they fail, interpret the experience with them.

Don't rescue them, but if they fall or fail, talk it over. Show them it's not the end of the world or a reflection on their identity. It's a chance to try again.

Tell them stories about your own struggles and failures.

My kids love to hear me talk about my past flops, failures, and fumbles. As we laugh together, they think, "Wow, if you did that and still made it, maybe there's hope for me."

Don't expect teachers to be nannies to your child.

As you interact with your child's teachers, don't ask them to give special favors or to be a second mom or dad. They are a good precursor to a boss at work.

Help them put their finger on something they really want to achieve.

Goals are important. They are targets to shoot for, and they are either hit or miss. Once you identify a goal, help them create a plan to reach it.

Establish rewards that require hard work and progress.

Separate the idea of merely showing up from putting out effort. Big difference. Set a reward they can receive only if they really excel.

Discuss your ambitions and how you felt when you accomplished them.

Once again, it's the power of stories. Talk about an ambition you had years ago, how you felt when you pursued it, and how rewarding it was inside to earn it.

Communicate your love and belief in them regardless of what happens.

Love should not be a reward for performing. Caring adults must demonstrate belief regardless of their accomplishments. This is a solid foundation for ambition.

Stop making excuses.

When they make a mistake, help them to own it. Don't teach them to blame others or make excuses. They must eventually learn that life isn't fair.

Fewer Rules...

So how do we correct this mistake of removing consequences for our kids' behavior? The quick and easy answer, of course, is to allow the consequences of bad decisions and wrong conduct to occur. But before you do this, think the issue through. The best way to do this is to make the experience instructive.

Kids in Generation iY have seldom had to delay gratification, and they've been given things that earlier generations had to work for. Why? I believe it's the messages permeating our culture. Parents hear, "The more you give your child, the better parent you are." Kids feel entitled to have what's advertised on TV and in movies. They hear, "This is the new cool thing. Everybody is getting it. If you don't have it, you're not cool." At school, on sports teams, or at home, students are rewarded for mediocre effort or for simply showing up. When they make a mistake, an adult often steps in and resolves it for them. Accordingly, their awareness of consequences is down and their sense of entitlement is up. Now the question is, how do we correct this predicament?

In this kind of world, creating a bunch of rules hasn't worked well. First, most students push back on rules. For that matter, the moment any of us are told we cannot or should not do something, the rebel inside us wants to do it. Second, rules haven't worked because we frequently fail to enforce them. We don't follow through. We threaten kids with a rule…then reduce the consequence. It's no wonder kids possess a sense of entitlement. We gave it to them.

…More Equations

Instead of a long list of rules, what if you began to share equations with your students at the beginning of a semester? Rather than saying, "No running in the hallway!" or "No cheating in the classroom!" consider an equation like this: "Doing ABC will result in this benefit, and doing XYZ will result in this consequence." And by the way, it works even better when students and adults adhere to the same equation.

It's all about behaviors and outcomes. I realize this may simply sound like a semantics issue, but it's far more than that. It's a way of helping students associate conduct with consequences, behavior with benefits. When a kid experiences a negative outcome, it isn't that the teacher doesn't like her or the dean has a vendetta against her. It's that she chose a course of action, and courses always have destinations. Actions always bring outcomes. That's how life works. If I jump off a 50-foot cliff, I will get hurt. Maybe die. I didn't get hurt because my teacher didn't like me or my parents wanted to make things hard for me. No, it's simply gravity at work. When I jump, gravity will pull me down. The law of gravity is an equation of life. It represents the relationship between action and outcome.

The best way to enter this lifestyle is to create agreements. Agreements feel a little like games to younger kids, and kids like games. Adults must be able to negotiate win/win agreements up front with their children to foster the right conduct. Usually kids are willing to keep fair agreements. The catch is, parents must be willing to follow through on the benefits and consequences of successful and failed agreements.

Jim Woodard works on our staff at Growing Leaders. He talks about how his mother raised her five children this way. This was one of her equations: "If you interrupt me while I'm talking on the phone, I will hang up the phone, and you will have to call the other person back and apologize for interrupting." It was an understandable equation, and she gave it with a smile. Jim recalled a couple of times when he barged into the house and interrupted his mom. She ended her call, and true to her word, Jim had to call the person back and apologize. He smiled as he told me, "I'm not sure if it was easier to call back when it was a friend or someone I didn't know. Either way, I stopped interrupting when she was on the phone."

Benefits and consequences are different from rewards and punishments. Consequences are the natural or agreed-upon results of an action or failure to act. The purpose of consequences is to remedy the negative results of behavior. Consequences reposition energy. Let's face it—punishment creates negative energy. Consequences may look the same on the outside, but they bring positive energy to repair or correct a negative situation.

Punishment looks backward. Consequences pay it forward. Remember the laws of physics—every action has an equal but opposite reaction. Benefits and consequences are simply part of that equation. This is simply how life works for children and for adults.

Starting the "Fewer Rules, More Equations" Lifestyle

Equations put the ball in your kids' court. You say, "If anyone does this, then that will happen. It's up to you. It's your choice." So in our home, my wife and I led things this way.

- We had very few rules. We cultivated a trusting relationship with our kids that reduced the need for them. We had only three or four rules.
- We communicated *many* equations to our kids. They

described various scenarios so that our kids always knew what destination each course of action led to.

- When either of our two kids faced some options, we sat down and talked about the outcomes, teaching them to think about benefits and consequences.
- When our kids were making a decision, we created fair agreements, including the outcomes of keeping the agreements or failing to do so.
- When either of our two kids chose a behavior, we sat down and debriefed the action and the outcome.

For example, when our son, Jonathan, turned 16, he wanted to move out to Hollywood to pursue an agent and some television work as an actor. I sat down with him and praised him for his ambition. Then we had a sobering conversation about the cost of such an endeavor, including the social, emotional, educational, and financial price tag. Economically, I decided I would split the cost with him. He would either get work out there or work when he returned home to pay for half the bills. At age 20 he finished his last payment. He's not angry with me about the payments—he's excited about what came of that venture. He got clear direction for his future. His sense of entitlement is low, his ambition is growing, and he's happy with his life. Why? He understood the equation going into it. This is the only way to set kids up for the world they'll enter as adults.

How about you? What rules could you transform into equations for your kids?

THE FURTHER OUT I LOOK, —— THE BETTER PARENTING DECISIONS I MAKE. ——

Short-term benefits often bring long-term consequences.
Short-term consequences often bring long-term benefits.

Sharon and Wade have three kids. The oldest is a special-needs daughter who requires much of Sharon's time and energy. Their youngest daughter, Brooke, is 14. One day, Brooke called to tell her mom she forgot to get a permission slip signed. Sharon listened empathetically as her daughter told her the consequences for not having the permission slip. The penalty was to run laps around the gym. Brooke was in tears and begged her mom to bring in the slip.

Sharon's response might sound cruel to you. "Brooke, honey, I feel horrible that you forgot to bring in the slip. I'm so sorry about this. I know it's embarrassing for you to have to run laps, but running will be good for you, and I bet you'll never forget to get a permission slip signed again. I'm busy right now and can't bring it in."

This was tough for Sharon because she loves her daughter. Driving five minutes to the school would have been easier than having that conversation. But Sharon is parenting for the long term, not the short term. And it's paying off. Brooke absolutely adores her mother. She respects her mom even more because she leads her so well. Brooke is a productive teen who works hard at home, does community service for her school, and serves on mission trips overseas with money she raises herself. Brooke is on her way to being a happy, healthy adult.

We Lie About Their Potential and Don't Explore Their True Potential

I know a young lady who's experiencing what her therapist calls a quarter-life crisis. Yep, you read that right. Not a midlife crisis, but a quarter-life crisis. She's twenty-five years old and seeing a counselor for depression and disillusionment.

When I spoke to her, she was very articulate. Eva told me that all her life she was told she was awesome. Her mother affirmed her brilliance at every turn on the soccer field, at piano recitals, in the classroom, and on the gymnastics floor. Eva regarded herself as a "smarty pants" and acknowledged that it felt good when adults praised her potential. The problem was, Eva went off to Georgia Tech following high school and soon met thousands of other smarty pants. They were every bit as sharp and gifted as she was. Suddenly her world crumbled. She wobbled through her years in college and then sought employment. She took two years to genuinely launch her career, and then it happened again. She was surrounded by smarty pants, just as she had been in college. Where did these people come from? How could so many gifted people converge in one place?

So Eva decided to push pause on her traditional job and pursue becoming a singer and musician. After all, her mother told her she was amazing at the piano and that she had the voice of an angel.

You can probably guess what happened. Eva soon discovered tens of thousands of her peers in the same spot. As she auditioned with loads of her colleagues, she clearly saw she was mediocre at best. Eva wasn't bad, she just wasn't someone who could make a career in show business. Hmm…where did all these talented people come from?

The answer is, they're everywhere.

In fact, you know this story. With each new season of *American Idol*, we watch hundreds if not thousands of fame-seeking young people stand in front of a panel of judges and try to perform. It's amusing. Sometimes hilarious. As you listen to some of the auditions, you want to ask them, "Who are your friends?"

So many of those young singers were lied to by parents and peers. They were told they should be on stage singing before millions of people, and they believed it. In fact, this is rampant today. In a nationwide survey, college students were asked, "What is your goal after college?" Their top two answers were to get rich and to become famous.

Sadly, this is a pipe dream for most. I'm not saying there's anything wrong with big dreams. I love kids with big dreams. I just want those kids to align their dreams with their true gifts, not with fame and glory.

How could so many adolescents today be this duped?

Just think about their world. They grew up with adults around them affirming their every turn, telling them…

- "Great job!" when they performed an effortless act.
- "You're amazing!" when they did only what was expected.
- "You're smart!" when they scored in the median range.
- "You're awesome!" when they simply did what they should.
- "You've got talent!" when they were good for their age but not great.

I know, I know…you're likely thinking, "What's the big deal? There's nothing wrong with praising our kids like this. I want them to feel confident and loved. I talk like this because I am so proud of them. It's normal, isn't it?"

Perhaps it is normal, but it's confusing our kids. Current studies show that when adult praise is over the top, when affirmation is exaggerated and not connected to reality, these things actually have a damaging effect. David Seamands wrote, "Children are the best recorders but the worst interpreters." Eva and her counseling sessions are not an isolated case. Hundreds of thousands of Evas are seeing therapists because they bought the lies adults told them growing up. It's not only sad—it's unnecessary. We lied to them and didn't know it.

My friend Greg Doss is an educator. He recently told me about Annie, a high school student who was ranked among the top five in her class. She always wanted to know who was ranked above her and how they could possibly be taking more AP classes than she was. It didn't surprise me to learn that Annie never received a grade below an A. If she ever did, she'd approach her teacher and get permission to resubmit the assignment. It always worked. Annie won awards and attended the governor's honor program in her state. Her GPA continued to climb. She told Greg that if she ever got a B on any project, she'd be devastated.

After graduation, Annie soon learned that postsecondary education is a completely different story. Upon receiving one of her first assignments back, she discovered she had failed it. Annie was shocked. Surely there must be some misunderstanding. She waited until after class to approach the instructor and negotiate. Politely, she asked if she could redo the assignment. The professor's reply was pointed: "This is college, not high school. There are no second chances. This is the real world."

As she spoke to my friend Greg, Annie was devastated. Her shock turned to grief and then to anger. But her anger wasn't directed at her college professor. She told Greg she was upset with her high school culture. "Teachers allowed us to keep doing assignments until we got the grade we wanted."

For the first time in her life, she had to adapt to the system rather than manipulate the system until it adapted to her. Annie's first year was a struggle, and she received her first B.

Like many other adolescents, Annie feels lied to.

Why Do We Do It?

You might be thinking, "Lies? Me? I would never lie to my children or my students or my young employees. I am an honest person."

You think so? Lying to our kids is rampant in our nation. It happens for a variety of reasons.

- *We're insecure.* Telling the truth, even gently, requires a deep level of emotional security. The kid we tell the truth to may reject us or may not like us enough to confide in us. We cannot let our need to be liked eclipse our pursuit of our children's best interests.

- *Speaking the truth takes time and work.* There may be only one truth but many ways to spin it. Sometimes we lie to get out of a jam. We can't handle the hassle. At times the lie just seems to make things easier.

- *The truth can be painful.* The truth can hurt and be much more painful than a charming lie, at least in the short run. To most of us, pain feels like an enemy. In the name of peace and harmony, we become spin doctors. We so want our kids to be happy, we sacrifice the truth in order to temporarily relieve the pain.

- *Facing the truth makes us responsible.* Lies sometimes let us off the hook. They allow us to pass the blame to someone else or avoid facing something we'd rather not acknowledge. Often we'd rather trade in long-term benefits for short-term ones.

- *We've lost sight of the truth ourselves.* We Baby Boomers or Gen Xers who are raising the next generation have our own set of misconceptions that can affect our ability to be truthful. Sometimes we tell lies because we believe them too.

The Problem with Distortion

I recognize I should probably use a euphemism for the word *lie*. It sounds so wrong, so harsh. We could replace the word *lie* by simply calling what we do *distorting the truth*. We want to introduce our kids to reality gently, so we withhold some of the truth. Whatever we call it, we still cause long-term problems by doing it. When we lie to our kids or distort things for them, disillusionment will follow the dreams that we helped them create—dreams that don't match their gifts. Consider how it leads to wrong conclusions.

- When we say they're smart, they assume school should require little effort.
- When we suggest they're amazing, they wonder why everyone doesn't adore them and want to be around them.
- When we tell them they're gifted, they get confused that people won't pay big money for their talent.
- When we say they're awesome at their sport, they don't understand why talent scouts don't recruit them.

We've actually developed a system that automatically sends mixed signals to kids as they mature. Parents drive cars with bumper stickers that say, My Kid Is Awesome. My Child Is Super Kid of the Month. My Kid Is an Honor Student. I even saw a bumper sticker that said, My Kid Is Better than Your Kid. We subtly send kids this message: "You're incredible. Just be nice. Stay within the boundaries, and you'll be rewarded." Then we place them in industrialized institutions that reinforce the delusion that their dreams should work out fine if they simply follow the rules, keep their nose clean, make a decent grade, and follow the advice of the career guidance counselor.

Uh, no. Not so much anymore.

Literary editor Rebecca Chapman was quoted in the *New York Times* as saying, "My whole life, I had been doing everything everyone told me. I went to the right school. I got really good grades. I got all the internships. Then, I couldn't do anything."[1]

She'd been handed the assumption that if you just do what the system tells you to do, it will all work out okay. That's not necessarily true. It's certainly not guaranteed—not in this economy. And our kids, the ones we love so much, deserve to know the truth.

Fifty years ago, life was more predictable. These were the top ten employers in the United States:

General Motors	Esso
Sears	General Electric
AT&T	Bethlehem Steel
A&P	US Steel
Ford	IT&T

These are the top ten employers today:

Walmart	Yum! (Taco Bell, KFC…)
Kelly Services	Target
IBM	Kroger
UPS	HP
McDonalds	The Home Depot

Of these ten companies, only two of them offer a path similar to what the vast majority of companies offered in 1960. In fact, I don't think there is just one path anymore. Most of our kids will not work for a massive company, making widgets. Nor do they want to. Many of our kids will have jobs that don't even exist today. These jobs will likely involve risk, uncertainty, faith, initiative, creativity, and lots of hard work.

And unlike childhood, there will likely be no guarantees. Seth Godin envisions the future awaiting our kids.

> What happens when there are fifty companies like Apple? What happens when there is an explosion in the number of new power technologies, new connection mechanisms, new medical approaches? The good jobs of the future aren't going to involve working for giant companies on an assembly line. They all require individuals willing to chart their own path, whether or not they work for someone else.

In my book *Generation iY: Our Last Chance to Save Their Future*, I suggest a handful of lies most parents pass on to their children. Here's one of the most popular: "You can do anything you want."

I recognize why we say this, but as our kids grow older, we must help them to see what we really meant. The line can't be taken literally. Unless they're athletically inclined, they will never play third base for the Boston Red Sox. Unless they have a tremendous voice, they will not become the next American Idol. At best, the line is a half-truth. We really meant, if they set their mind to do something, they'll be amazed at what they can pull off. The catch is, it needs to be something within their gift area. They cannot simply make up a dream or copy a friend's dream and call it theirs. Dreams should be attached to strengths. Again, we must relay the truth to our children.

THE PRINCIPLE

When we distort the truth about our kids' potential,
their dreams won't match their gifts,
and disillusionment will follow.

Let's look at the numbers and see how our distortions have harmed our kids.

Depression and Anxiety

We live in complex times. As I work with thousands of parents and faculty members each year, I'm increasingly convinced that adults who care about kids today are more engaged than at any time since I began my career in 1979. Simultaneously, however, I'm observing a more troubled population of kids, especially by the time they reach their teen years. At first, this appears to be an oxymoron. How can such a cared-for generation experience such emotional difficulties?

When parents raise their kids on large doses of affirmation, they initially create a positive environment for them. Lots of happiness and warm fuzzies. As the kids grow older, reality hits. They realize Mom is the only one telling them they're awesome. By high school, anxiety surfaces for millions of them. They have a cell phone, a laptop, a Facebook page, and a Twitter account, but they're lonely and depressed. They question what they've been told and who they really are. We would have served them better by speaking more honestly to them when they were young children.

Unrealistic and Unmet Expectations

Both parents and teachers unwittingly lie to the kids. Parents may lie to them to secure their kids' self-esteem. The problem is, after decades of the self-esteem movement, we've come to recognize that exaggerated compliments do not build self-esteem. Flattery cultivates narcissism. Kids become self-absorbed. At the beginning of this chapter, we met a young person experiencing a quarter-life crisis. In 2001, Alexandra Robbins and Abby Wilner, in their book *Quarterlife Crisis*, described the growing number of people who were slipping into critical depression because they didn't make their first million dollars, find the perfect spouse, or get the perfect job by the time they were 25. Of course, we tell them, "You're only 25!" But we'd already given them unrealistically high expectations for how quickly and easily they would become superstars. We did them a disservice. In chapter 3 we saw a term that therapists now use when diagnosing many teens: "high arrogance, low self-esteem." It's a pitiful, unnecessary state of feeling cocky because they've been told they're great, but deep down they suspect it may not be true.

Wandering Instead of Working

When kids fail to get a handle on the truth about their potential, they graduate from high schools or colleges and still have no idea what to do. So as we've seen, many of them move back home. In a time when they should be launching their careers, they are languishing. Instead of working, they are wandering.

Today, parents overwhelmingly believe their children should go to college. But according to higher-education faculty feedback, more than half should not. Certainly, all high school graduates need to prepare for their careers, but for many, a liberal arts degree in college just isn't the right way to do it. Edward Gordon, an internationally recognized expert on education reform and the future of the labor market, makes this clear.

> Many economists believe that 70 percent of the good jobs
> in the current and future American economy will not

require a four-year college degree; rather, they will require some form of additional training and education such as an associate's degree or technical training certificate.[2]

To be blunt, work is the best truth teller of all. Employment furnishes us with honest feedback about our character, our work ethic, our willingness to serve, our passions, and our ability to control our attitudes. Jobs are like mirrors—they reflect all our features and flaws. This is why I often tell kids that it doesn't matter if they start at the bottom of the career ladder as long as they're on the right ladder. Work turns theory into practice. It does wonders to mature them.

If we aren't truthful about our kids' potential, we create expectations that are either too high or too low. Again, I'm all for dreaming big—but within their gifting and not for the purpose of becoming rich or famous. Those are by-products of performing well. Sadly, so many 18-year-old students are misplaced or displaced. Numerous colleges report that a mere 18 percent of their freshmen class actually graduate. This is often an unnecessary waste of time and money.

Wishing They Were Someone Else

When we distort the truth about kids' potential, they can lose their way. Without clarity on who they are, they get distracted and begin copying others. They may explore future possibilities but deviate from their gifts and identity, trying to become someone else. Have you noticed a trend in our culture, especially over the past ten years? Films come out every year illustrating someone's addiction to other people, such as *The Bling Ring*, a 2013 story of our growing obsession with celebrities and their scandalous lives.

Ironically, this obsession clouds these kids' vision. Instead of building ambition, it reduces it. Recently, high school students were asked, "What would you most like to be in your career?" The top answers they chose may surprise you.

a chief of a major company (9.5 percent)

a Navy SEAL (9.8 percent)

a United States senator (13.6 percent)

a personal assistant to a famous celebrity (43.4 percent)

Becoming an assistant to a celeb was their top answer—by far! Kids don't want the pressure of being a performer; they just want to be close to someone who lives that fairy-tale lifestyle.

Online games like Second Life continue to attract attention among young people. These games allow users to pose as someone else and live different lives with other homes, cars, and possessions. They get to live vicariously through an avatar. The game preys on kids' preoccupation with pretending to be someone else, to be a star.

None of these realities are mortifying. But they illustrate this generation's growing preoccupation with fame, with being someone else, someone who seems to have a better life. I'm not sure whether this expanding consumption is the result of kids overdosing on other people's Facebook pages, Instagrams, and Tweets and becoming envious of their lifestyles. Regardless, kids seem to believe their lives are boring when compared to other people's.

What's wrong with this scenario?

It's an irony, but in a day of bloating self-absorption, these kids don't like their own lives enough to be content with them. They're not glitzy enough. Many young people have bought into the notion that anything boring is bad. Routines are blue-collar. They want their lives to sparkle. I believe anyone's life can sparkle plenty *without being famous* if they choose to invest their time and energy well. But we have to help kids shift their focus to who they really are and what gifts they have to offer the world around them.

Exploring Their True Potential: Your To-Do List

Of course, your kids may be highly gifted. Perhaps they should pursue some incredible calling in life. I am only trying to ensure they aren't led astray by your idea or a friend's idea of who they are and what they should do. They are loaded with potential to serve people and solve problems. That's what leaders do. And it's up to us to help them get ready for this calling. The future awaits them.

Almost every time I do a parenting event, people ask me about the top things we've done for our kids to get them ready for life. I don't claim to be a parenting guru, but here's my response to the question.

I focused on the following messages the first five years and the last five years they lived at home.

As I mentioned in chapter 3, I believe the things parents communicate the first five years of their children's lives and the last five years they are at home are paramount. These are worth reviewing here.

By communication I don't merely mean words. I mean the messages we send through our lives, conversations, time, associations, and priorities. Their first five years, they must embrace these messages:

> You are loved.
>
> You are safe.
>
> You are valuable.
>
> You are uniquely gifted.
>
> You are supported.

Once kids are secure in those messages, they're free to risk and explore who they're meant to be—their strengths, their passions, and the contexts that capture their imagination. Built on this foundation, they can handle the more challenging teen messages. I believe the five years before they leave home, the messages must change.

> Life is difficult.
>
> You are not in control.
>
> You are not that important.
>
> Your life is not about you.
>
> You're going to die one day and leave a legacy.

I exposed them to people who helped them discover their strengths.

While our kids were growing up, my wife and I took time to introduce them to significant leaders who were in careers that matched our kids' interests. Both Bethany and Jonathan met actors, business executives, moms, artists, writers, pastors, and counselors who provided wisdom as they discovered their own gifts. This was immensely helpful. It built their self-esteem, and it prevented them from venturing too far down the wrong path. Our kids went to lunch with adults, traveled to meet them, and interviewed them so these leaders could model the way for them. Both our daughter and son did much of this before they left for college. Taking time after high school to work and to explore their talents and values prepared them well for higher education. They had an advantage over their peers. They knew who they were.

I provided a rite of passage experience for them.

Probably the best decision I made as a parent was to provide an experience for my kids when they turned 13. Bethany and Jonathan each took a one-year journey, meeting with key mentors and learning life principles on location that affirmed their identity and equipped them to transition from childhood to adulthood.

Bethany met with six marvelous women (whom she helped choose). She got a "heart full of wisdom" as she accompanied them to their workplaces, their homes, and their places of community service. Jonathan and I met with men from various backgrounds who provided experiences on what it meant to become a man. At the end of the year, both my kids participated in an event where the mentors they met with affirmed and admonished them and celebrated their entrance into manhood and womanhood. Huge payoff. (I outline the details in my book *Generation iY: Our Last Chance to Save Their Future*.)

I encouraged them to take a "gap year."

Both of my kids took a "gap year" once they finished high school and before they entered college. They didn't do this because they felt unready for higher education. They did it to gain experience they could not get in a school. Gap years are popular in Europe, and they are becoming more popular in the United States. My teens spent the year working at Growing Leaders, the nonprofit organization I lead. They did it because they knew that a year of working, traveling, meeting new people, and exploring the real world would prepare them to invest their time and my money wisely once they hit the university campus. Both Bethany and Jonathan matured incredibly during that 12-month period and entered college prepared for its rigor.

Six Ambitions to Cultivate: Their To-Do List

As I close this chapter, let me suggest six ambitions I've tried to build into my kids over the years. These may be great targets for your kids to aim for as well. Each is followed by a popular quote.

Know yourself.

Nothing is more pitiful than adults still trying to figure out who they are. We must expose kids to environments where they can experiment with who they really are—from the inside out. What do they enjoy doing? When do they feel comfortable? Where do they flourish and make their best contribution?

"Our worst sins arise out of our innate fear that we are nobody."

Develop your gift.

Often people spend most of their time working on their weaknesses and little time sharpening their strengths. The problem is, a weakness won't grow beyond average. Each kid has a primary motivational gift. We must help them find the "hub" gift around which their other gifts revolve.

"Everyone must discover their strengths—their natural talents, spiritual gifts, and acquired skills."

Value people.

Along the way, kids must discover that people aren't means to an end—they are the end. Adding value to people and prioritizing them over projects or possessions is a sign of maturity. Teens often value popularity or pleasure. We must help them see the significance of serving people.

"It is only in developing others that we truly succeed."

Find your passion.

We must help kids identify the issue that fires them up inside, the one that motivates them more than anything else. Everyone has been created with at least one passion. Some have more than one. We must fan their passion into a productive flame. Unfortunately, many never discover their passion.

"Find a job you're passionate about, and you'll never work a day in your life."

Learn perseverance.

Today, kids have short attention spans. They have a "Google reflex" and quit when things don't work quickly. Watch closely and you'll discover they often catch a disease of the mind. You might call it *excusitus*. We must prevent them from making excuses and model for them the importance of sticking with their commitments until the end.

"It takes twenty years to be an overnight success."

Pursue excellence.

It's so easy for youth to have a "good enough" mentality. Good leaders introduce them to excellence. Most kids don't perform excellently on their own. We must help raise the bar for them in at least one area of their life and help them know what excellence feels like.

"When we strive for excellence, we find that all kinds of resources follow that pursuit."

I'm not suggesting that you push your kids into a performance trap. We obviously need to communicate to them that they're valued and loved just for who they are. But I'm concerned we are not intentional enough about balancing our love with the challenge for them to stretch and become the best version of themselves.

I recently read a story of a Chinese student that stopped me in my tracks. In fact, when I read about the attitude of this young woman in China, I realized I'd seen a real picture of what pursuing one's potential could look like. It's the story of a severely disabled girl who refused to make excuses for not growing and learning. She's become a model for everyone in the city of Hong Kong and in all of China.

Tsang Tsz-Kwan is blind and severely hearing impaired, and she has limited sensitivity in her fingers. Her parents have attempted to balance their unconditional love with a tenacity to not settle for anything less than what she is capable of—even with multiple handicaps. They knew she had potential. When she tried to use her fingers to read in Braille, she just couldn't make out the letters. Instead of giving up on reading, however, the 20-year-old has taught herself how to read Braille *with her lips*.[3]

You read that right. She now is an avid reader and student.

The story doesn't end there. CNN reported she has met great success—Tsang scored within the top 5 percent in almost all of her subjects in Hong Kong's college entrance examination. Because of her disabilities, she could have opted not to take the tests, according to the South China *Morning Post*. But she decided that wasn't an option. She will not make excuses for herself.

> "I have to accept I'm disadvantaged…I decided to take the challenge whatever the results," she told the paper. "I think the most important thing is the courage to face the challenge…The inconveniences and limitations [my impairments] bring will follow me my whole life…and I must have the courage to face the facts…I'm going to treasure what I still have."[4]

So, what's our excuse for not reaching our potential? What's our children's excuse for not reaching their potential?

We Won't Let Them Struggle or Fight

The *New York Post* has become famous for exposing the most bizarre parenting habits in our nation. In 2013, it reported how wealthy parents were spending far too much money to teach their children entirely the wrong lesson. Some of their case studies were real gems.

For instance, several moms have figured out a way to cut the long lines at Walt Disney World. They shamelessly hire disabled people to pose as family members so they and their kids can jump to the front of the line and not have to wait. The "black market Disney guides" run $130 an hour or $1040 for an entire day. After all, no child should be inconvenienced by a long line.[1]

Other parents (in the same tax bracket, I'm sure) are now hiring "recreation experts" for $400 an hour to teach preschoolers how to play with friends. Wow. As a kid, I had to learn this all by myself. As Tara Palmeri reports, "Child's play is deadly serious for parents, because the toddlers will be judged on these skills when they apply to top-end schools."[2]

Still other parents hire "child helpers" when they are too busy to do things for their own kids. These helpers run all kinds of errands, from taking forgotten backpacks to school to returning the outfit at the mall that was a size too small.

Our great-grandparents would turn over in their graves if they heard this.

Overfunctioning

My guess is that you smiled as you read these accounts. For most of us, the scenarios are inconceivable. But our lives may be only slightly different. We may not have a child helper, recreation expert, or a disabled guide, but we often overparent our children these days. Child experts call what we do *overfunctioning*.

Overfunctioning in parenting simply means doing too much for our children, intervening and removing common struggles they may experience in their day. We intervene in our kids' everyday lives because we know they're stressed-out by an overscheduled week of classes and activities. We hate to see them struggle and become frustrated. We feel if we just help them a bit, we can ease their struggle. Isn't that what good parents do?

We've seen that American parents view pain as a negative thing. The same is true with struggle. We have created a world of conveniences, filled with smartphones, microwaves, Internet shopping, and online banking. The subtle message is that struggles are to be avoided. We want as much convenience as possible. In fact, we feel entitled to it.

But we fail to see that when we remove the struggles from our children's lives, we begin to render them helpless. They don't have the opportunity to develop the life skills they'll need later on. Further, when we step in to control their levels of struggle, they don't learn how to be in control or under control themselves. In fact, all they learn is how to be controlled. Hmm…I don't think that's all we want our kids to know as adults.

When we remove struggles, we actually do more harm than the struggles would have caused. Kids lose the opportunity to develop resilience, creativity, and problem-solving skills. We actually train young people to need help every step of the way. Before we observe the research on this, take a look at how this works in the games and toys our kids are using.

What the Trends in Games Teach Us About Kids Today

I've been watching a trend that I believe every teacher, parent, coach, youth pastor, and school administrator should be watching these days. It's the changes toy makers have made in board games to engage today's kids.

In 2013, Hasbro reported it lost more than $2 million during one quarter, compared to a $17 million profit in that same period in 2012. That's enough to make any executive rethink their product.[3]

So, like many others, Hasbro has begun adjusting their toys and games to fit today's generation of kids, who are…well, different from past generations of kids, who grew up in a slower, less convenient time, when kids were more likely to play outside.

For example, when I was growing up, the game of Monopoly could go on for hours, maybe even days among family members. Families would leave the board out on the kitchen table so they could continue the next evening. Consumer research reveals that kids want to play Monopoly faster these days. So Monopoly is making some changes. First, Monopoly Millionaire is now in stores. The first person to accumulate a million dollars wins the game. Second, Monopoly is doing away with Go to Jail cards. In fact, there's no jail at all anymore. Kids don't have the time or patience to spend time in jail. They want to keep moving forward.

Recently, Lego made some changes too. Do you remember playing with Legos when you were growing up? I do. I had a big box of those little bricks and built stuff for hours in my room. Today, Legos have undergone a change. Seeing a dip in sales, the Lego Group decided to include instructions in the product, telling kids exactly what to build and how to build it. They've found it fits the "I need you to spoon-feed me the answer" mindset adults have created in kids today.

A new version of the game of Life lets players use an iPad touchscreen as a high-tech spinner and then watch a video to see the results of their "life decision." John Frascotti of Hasbro reports the company is introducing several new gaming innovations this year that will feature this convergence of analog and digital play—both a board and a screen. You already know that Transformers toys have been transformed into two box-office hit movies over the past five years. It's now both in a box and on a screen.

What's Our Takeaway?

Kids in Generation iY want experiences that include…

- *Speed.* "I get bored easily. Keep the pace of change high."
- *Screens.* "I am visual. I'm more comfortable looking at pixels than at people."
- *Stipulations.* "I need you to prescribe what you want me to do."
- *Stimulation.* "I need quick rewards and outside payoffs to keep me engaged."

It's important for us to understand today's young people, but it's also important to recognize what we've done to them. Have we done too much? In our effort to keep them happy and entertained, have we sabotaged their ability to persevere, bounce back, learn soft skills, and find internal motivation? Perhaps it's time to reignite their imagination, ask them to make up the game, and help them learn how to wait for prizes that come from being committed to a goal.

We can understand why parents want to comfort their kids and remove all their struggles. But struggling is part of growing up. So we must overcome our innate desire to remove the obstacles in our kids' lives, or we'll have aging, immature young adults on our hands. Dr. Aaron Sterns provides an excellent summary.

> To attain emotional maturity each of us must learn to develop two critical capacities: the ability to live with uncertainty and the ability to delay gratification in favor of long-range goals. Adolescence is a time of maximum resistance to further growth. It is a time characterized by the teenager's ingenious efforts to maintain the privileges of childhood, while at the same time demanding the rights of adulthood. It is a point beyond which many humans do not pass emotionally. The more we do for our children, the less they can do for themselves. The dependent child of today is destined to become the dependent parent of tomorrow.

THE PRINCIPLE

When we eliminate challenges and difficulties from their lives, kids are conditioned to give up easily without trying.

What Happens When We Remove Their Struggles?

When we do what seems to be natural—intervene and remove the struggle from our kids' lives—we actually create worse struggles for them later.

Research from the University of Mary Washington reveals that when parents intervene too much in their children's lives, they hinder the kids from learning to get along with others. Additionally, the study reports the children are prone to become depressed, feel less competent to manage life, and live less satisfied lives.[4]

How could this be? Consider what your children experience during adolescence. They naturally desire more autonomy. It is normal for them to want to spread their wings, try out their skills, and find where they belong. In fact, it would be strange if they didn't experience this yearning. When we try to help them by removing any struggles, we emasculate them. We unwittingly deem them incompetent.

Truth be told, parents must assess their level of intervention and involvement in their children's lives as they age. Maturity doesn't happen automatically. We must let kids mature. We can both stunt their maturity and foster it. Children's need for autonomy increases with time, so parents must adapt and adjust their level of control and involvement as kids strive to become independent young adults.

When our children were young, my wife and I found ourselves picking up their toys for them, putting their clothes away, and even fetching a ball that rolled away when they were fully capable of doing these things themselves. We weren't noticing the patterns we were establishing. As we became aware, we may have looked uncaring to onlookers at first. But we knew we had to condition our kids to expect to get the ball for themselves or to put their clothes and toys away. In fact, preparing them to do this was a superior method for demonstrating our care and concern for them. We were building an expectation and an ability for them to do it for themselves. They have since become more self-reliant adults because they are self-sufficient.

When we talked about this change, my wife confessed something I believe many parents fall prey to as they raise their kids. She told me that doing so much for the kids met an emotional need in her own life. We all need to feel needed. When we remove struggles in our kids' lives, they begin to expect and need us to continue to do so. In fact, the cycle is addictive. Deep down, we like that addiction.

Psychologist Debbie Pincus writes, "If a parent's emotional needs are met through their child, essentially they are tying her shoes for her every step of the way."[5]

Generation on a Tightrope

What does this do to our kids in school? One of the top complaints I hear from teachers in both K-12 and higher education is that students constantly tell them, "I can't do this. It's too hard."

Unfortunately, though our kids make up the most educated generation in American history, they consistently need help as they go off to college. They are frequently unready for hard work. Few have ever struggled in school. Some have never studied. Dr. Arthur Levine reports that in a recent undergraduate survey, the proportion of students taking remedial courses steadily increased from 1969 to 2009 in 99 percent of colleges. Further, 54 percent of students report that their classes are difficult or very difficult.[6] The California State University system, for example, admits the top third of the state's high school seniors. Yet six out of ten of them have to take remedial classes. Half are not academically prepared for college.[7] Are students really not as smart as their counterparts years ago? I don't think so. We've simply tried to remove the struggle in the years preceding college.

Let me be clear. I do believe there are exceptions to this rule. But nationwide, the trend is clear. Many students tell university professors they've never learned to study. They have slipped through high school without much homework at all. Somehow, adults have backed down when students declare, "This is too hard."

This problem dates back 60 years when educational pedagogy began to change. In 1953, C.W. Washburn wrote an article titled "Adjusting the Program to the Child," questioning the long-standing practice that all kids could learn things the same way at the same age if they tried hard enough. His article cited several schools that attempted to adjust coursework to meet the wide range of differences in student development. This later became known as "differentiated instruction," or DI.[8] He wanted to move from the industrial model, which he felt was a cookie-cutter system, to one that was tailored for each child. In principle, I totally agree. Unfortunately, over the decades the result has become what today's teachers consider too much of a good thing. They report…

- Teachers are spoon-feeding kids too much, resulting in an inability to apply what they've learned.

- The students' ownership of the material isn't being developed because we're making all kinds of adaptations for them.

- Differentiation is shortchanging our students of critical skills, soft skills, resilience, and problem-solving abilities.

- Students lose their incentive to push themselves, knowing teachers will be reteaching rather than having them apply what they know.[9]

The sad part is, there is no existing empirical evidence that DI has a positive impact on student achievement. It was well-intentioned, but we actually reduced the academic stamina of our kids. They are banking on us to grade on a curve.

Unfortunately, as I've stated, children who avoid stressful situations are more likely to develop anxiety, according to an analysis of parent and child surveys conducted by Mayo Clinic researchers. The underlying theory isn't new—an absence of risk and challenge in childhood leads to nervousness and anxiety later on. But researchers were surprised that their surveys on avoidance had the ability to predict which children would develop more anxiety a year later.

The researchers asked parents to respond to questions like this: "When your child is scared or worried about something, does he or she ask to do it later?" And they asked children to respond to statements like this: "When I feel scared or worried about something I try not to go near it." Children who said they avoided scary situations tended to post higher anxiety scores when they were surveyed again 8 to 12 months later. "That was consistent with the model for how anxiety disorders develop," said lead author Stephen Whiteside, a pediatric psychologist with the Mayo Clinic Children's Center. "Kids who avoid fearful situations don't have the opportunity to face their fears and don't learn that fears are manageable."[10]

The researchers also tracked anxious children and found their avoidance behaviors declined substantially after receiving "exposure therapy." This form of therapy gradually exposes kids to things they avoid and helps them manage their fears. The fact that these children were no longer nervous about these things was a strong indicator that the kids were getting control of their fears.

Let Them Struggle So They Can Be Strong

In June 2012, an article appeared in *MoneyWatch* titled, "Why my child will be your child's boss." The title alone arrested me and enticed me to read it. The piece covered a parent's discovery of a teacher in her child's three- to four-year-old play group placing a saw—the kind you buy at a hardware store—on the ground for the kids to play with. In the United States, this would result in the teacher being fired or charged with child endangerment. Here's the parent's report.

> But this happened not in the U.S. but in Switzerland, where they believe children are capable of handling saws at age 3 and where kindergarten teachers counsel parents to let their 4- and 5-year-olds walk to school alone. "Children have pride when they can walk by themselves," the head of

the Muenchenstein, Switzerland, Kindergartens said last week at a parent's meeting, reminding those in attendance that after the first few weeks of school children should be walking with friends, not their mom…

I tried to hide my American-bred fear and casually asked a teacher about her procedures in case of emergencies. She rattled them off to me…but added, "I've been a forest play-group teacher for 10 years, and I've never had to call a parent because of an injury."

What's a "forest" teacher?…That alludes to a tradition here that we signed our 3-year-old up for. Every Friday, whether rain, shine, snow, or heat, he goes into the forest for four hours with 10 other children. In addition to playing with saws and files, they roast their own hot dogs over an open fire…

The leadership at many American companies were raised in a similar way to the Swiss children in my neighborhood. Boys had pocketknives. Everyone rode bikes to school. Kids started babysitting other children at 11 or 12 years old. Now? We coddle and protect and argue with teachers when our little darlings receive anything worse than an A on a paper.

The result? Well, the preliminary results from this method of parenting are hitting the workforce now. They are poor communicators who insist on using text-speak. Their mothers are calling employers. They believe they should be given rewards and promotions for the act of showing up to work on time.

If this trend in the U.S. continues, American children will become more crippled in their ability to make their own decisions (Mom is always around), manage risk (at what age do you become magically able to use a saw?) or overcome a setback (you learn nothing when Mom and Dad sue the school district to get your grade changed).

By contrast, my son learns about risk management every week. He'll be in a school system that has no qualms about holding a child back if he doesn't understand the material. And "helicopter" parenting? Not tolerated by the schools or the other mothers at the playground.

So, while he's 4 and generally covered in dirt, I suspect he'll be more prepared for leadership when we move back to the U.S. than will children who have no freedom and responsibility and face no consequences.[11]

Correcting Four Mistakes We Make with Kids

Kids are growing up in a world that's very different from the one I grew up in. Both teachers and parents have changed the way they approach leading students. Some of these changes are great, but some have had unintended consequences.

Social scientists agree that kids today are highly confident and believe they can change the world. Unfortunately, there have been some unintended consequences to our new leadership style.

Adults won't let kids fail.

I introduced this in chapter 1. Think about this change. In the past, when a student got in trouble or failed a class, parents reinforced the teacher's grade and insisted the student study harder. Today, parents often side with their child, and the teacher gets in trouble. Moms and dads have made their children their trophies. Children have become a reflection of the parents' success. So every kid is a winner, they all get trophies, we pass them on to the next grade even if they're not really ready for it, we will graduate them even if they didn't learn a subject, and we give them money even if they didn't earn it. Obviously, this is not how life works after childhood.

What can we do? Identify opportunities to allow your young person to take calculated risks and experience failure on a project or in a class. Coach them but don't intervene and do it for them. Let them build emotional muscle that is capable of enduring a failure and seeing that they can live through it—that there really is life afterward.

Adults won't let kids fall.

In many ways we've refused to allow our kids to be harmed emotionally or physically. Helmets. Knee pads. Safety belts. More kids play inside with structured virtual games than outside where they can get hurt. This makes sense, but consider the potential damage in the long run. The truth is, kids need to fall a few times to learn it's normal. Teens likely need to break up with a boyfriend to appreciate the emotional maturity that lasting relationships require. Pain is actually a necessary teacher. It is a part of health and maturity.

What can we do? First of all, don't rescue kids from all harm. Guide them, coach them, and advise them on how to handle difficult times—but allow them the struggle of working their way through the process. Give them some freedom. Just as a butterfly must fight its way out of the cocoon in order to be strong enough to fly, young people must build emotional strength through hardship. No pain, no gain.

Recently, friends of ours were outside with their eight-year-old son. As we talked, their boy fell off the swing and began to cry. Instead of panicking, his mother calmed him, nursed his small wound, and told him he would be okay. Then she shared how she had skinned her knee as a little girl and everything healed up just fine. Instantly, his tears dried up, and he smiled and went back to playing.

Adults won't let kids fear.

Many adults want to prevent their children from ever experiencing fear. Now, don't get me wrong—fear can be a paralyzing emotion. I know adults who are crippled by all kinds of fears—fear of flying, heights, strange places…you name it. Today, adults are afraid kids will be abducted, poisoned, bitten, or even shot. This fear became pronounced after the Columbine High School massacre in April 1999. Parents yanked their children out of public schools and enrolled them in private schools or homeschooled them. We didn't want them harmed on our watch, so we decided to remove any possible cause of fear.

This was naturally passed on to the kids. Young people became accustomed to guaranteed outcomes. In the end, they knew everything would work out fine. But again, if kids never learn to handle fear, they may be unable to cope with it as adults, when no one is around to help them. Our homes and schools are havens of guarantees, insurance policies, and warranties. We want to guarantee outcomes and remove all fear of consequences. We want reassurance, which real life doesn't really grant.

Psychologists tell us that people are born with only two fears—the fear of falling and of loud noises. We accumulate the rest of our fears over time. However, the best way to beat a fear is to face it, to get back on the horse after falling off. This empowers a person to not fear the horse.

The next time your children mention being afraid, talk about it. Encourage them to take small steps to overcome it. Further, the next time you are tempted to remove a task or project because it scares your children, think again. Tell them and show them how to face fears. In fact, why not identify one and create a plan to overcome it by "running to the roar"? My son and I did this when he hesitated to get his driver's license five years ago. The plan involved both conversations and actions, and it worked. He moved quickly from driving in safe parking lots to navigating freeways. It was fulfilling to watch.

Adults won't let kids fight.

Let me clarify what I *don't* mean by this term. I'm not suggesting parents, teachers, and coaches should allow young people to get into fights with each other. In fact, we need to teach the opposite to our kids—how to collaborate and work as a team.

However, life requires a certain struggle in order for us to grow and feel good about ourselves. Facing and overcoming adversity builds self-esteem and conditions us to be strong enough for what lies ahead. Opposition and hardship force us to reach down and pull out the very best that lies within us. Conflict can actually make us stronger.

Sadly, I hear of more and more schools that are removing this necessary element from the classroom. I spoke with a teacher who said she was no longer allowed to use the word *no* in her classroom. It was too negative. We've already seen that some schools have banned red ink when grading papers (too harsh!) and some parents are asking school superintendents to do away with grades (too discouraging!). I understand the intent of parents and teachers who suggest such moves, but I cannot help but be burdened by the fact that this shrinks the very emotional muscles kids must build to thrive. If the butterfly could talk, he would tell you the struggle to break out of the cocoon gives him the strength to fly.

What can we do? Pause and think before you talk to or provide direction for your students. It's normal to want to remove hardship from our kids' lives, but it's not in their best interests. They need us to be responsive to them and demanding of them at the same time. When they face conflict or adversity, don't remove it. Talk them through it. Encourage them that they have what it takes to overcome it. Brainstorm a game plan to beat it.

I know a high school girl who got a bad grade on a science test. She wanted her mom to contact the teacher and ask her to change the grade. Instead, the mom explained how that wouldn't help her in college. Then she told her daughter how she'd gotten a couple of bad grades in science—it led her to seek out a tutor, and her grades improved. She then told her daughter she'd be glad to help her find a tutor to help raise her grades. A simple, commonsense response. Brilliant.

Earlier, I compared this process to a butterfly emerging from a cocoon. I remember seeing a cocoon in my backyard when I was kid, playing with my friend Jay. We took it down from the tree, laid it on our driveway, and watched for that little fellow to spring out. After 15 minutes and no action, I looked at Jay and told him it needed help. I gently pried open the cocoon just a bit, and a leg poked out. Eureka! We waited some more, and after another 10 minutes, I decided I needed to help the butterfly again. I pried it open further and did this three more times over the next 30 minutes. Finally the opening was big enough for the creature to crawl out. But that's just it. It was a creature and not a butterfly that crawled out. He was dark and deformed, and he never flew. I believe he died by the end of the day.

Hmm…how could this happen? I was helping the little guy, wasn't I?

You already know the answer. My help really wasn't help at all. I appeared to be helping, but when I removed the struggle, I took away his opportunity to build enough strength to push his way out and fly. In the end, I actually removed his ability to fly.

May we never do this to our kids. Charles Lindbergh said, "What kind of man would live where there is no daring? I don't believe in taking foolish chances, but nothing can be accomplished if we don't take any chances at all."

We Give Them What They Should Earn

Aubrey is a young lady who desperately wants to be on her own and to learn to make her own choices. Unfortunately, this 21-year-old student at the University of Cincinnati has parents who claim they care so much for her, they can't let her do that. So in January 2013, Aubrey Ireland got a restraining order on her parents for stalking her.

I know it sounds crazy, but it's true.

> Ireland told the court that despite making the dean's list, her parents would routinely drive 600 miles from Kansas to Ohio to make unannounced visits to her at school. They...installed keylogging software on her computer and cell phone to keep track of her every move.[1]

Aubrey even reported that her mother wanted to stay on Skype all night with her, basically to watch her sleep. All her life, they've been doing things for their daughter, so they felt their actions were only logical. After all, she belonged to them.

Sometimes parents just don't know when to let go. The student told the court, "I was a dog with a collar on."

Her parents soon could not get within 500 feet of her, and due to this order, they're requesting the school pay back the tuition they've spent on their daughter. It's now a battle. They accused her of drug abuse, promiscuity, and mental illness—they believe she needs them to watch her. It won't surprise you that Aubrey is an only child.

The problem is, Aubrey is learning to be on her own the hard way.

Helicopter parents aren't new. For years they've ignored boundaries and embarrassed their kids. Sometimes they even do this at their child's workplace.

> In June 2012, researchers at the College of Business and Economics at West Virginia University conducted a study of 340 students and found that many simply grow accustomed to parents' constant involvement. Nearly 7 out of 10 students said it was "somewhat" or "very appropriate" to receive help from their parents writing a résumé or a cover letter. One-fifth of students thought it was fine to have their parents contact a prospective employer.[2]

Wow.

Very often, kids enjoy this parenting style. And why not? Their parents are doing things that spare them the hassle of working or striving or achieving. Most kids will take the big favor from us parents. Who wouldn't want a personal assistant? The problem is, when kids get used to this overparenting, they become dependent. They get so used to it, they develop no resilience or ambition or work ethic. They get stuck.

On the other hand, some kids see what's happening to them. Like Aubrey, they attempt to break the umbilical cord and launch out on their own. This can meet with resistance, both from within and without. Inwardly, the kids are unprepared for the future. And outwardly, they bump up against Mom or Dad when they try to spread their wings. Instead of seeing independence as a positive sign of maturing, helicopter parents resent the idea of self-sufficiency in their children, perceiving that they're acting ungrateful.

Why Do Parents Hover like This?

As a dad, I understand the desire to want the best for my kids, to want them to be safe, and to want them to have all the advantages possible as they leave home. Yet far too often our desire takes the form of giving our children what they should earn. Even when kids are fully capable of working for a paycheck, earning a scholarship, or achieving a goal, we step in and just give it to them. We feel it is our right and our duty. As I mentioned before, this is a big change in parental values since my childhood. Rather than taking pride in giving their children whatever they need, parents now take pride in giving them whatever they want. In fact, we often feel we're poor parents if we don't give them what they want. Why do we do this? Let me share some of my speculations.

- We have an ego. We look bad if we fall short of fulfilling their desires.
- We compare ourselves to other parents.
- We are control freaks. We don't trust things will work out without our help.
- We fear they're unready. They appear unprepared to do things on their own.
- We have our own emotional needs. Our baggage makes us need to be needed.

Let me illustrate what this looks like in everyday life. Shannon is a teen who enjoys wearing name-brand clothes. Like most girls, she'd rather not wear anything else. Unfortunately, Shannon has no job, so she can't afford those clothes. Instead of letting Shannon learn to go without until she can earn enough to pay for them, Mom gladly buys them for her. Shannon is happy for now, but she is not developing the ability to delay gratification. This makes her less attractive to girl-friends and to guys (she's a bit of a brat) and to coaches (she has no discipline). One day when she's forced to get a job, her ramp-up time may be enormous.

Heath is a good kid, but he hasn't worked a day in his life. As a teen, he wants toys that are bigger than those he played with as a young child—cars, smartphones, and digital video equipment. Those toys are…well, expensive. During his childhood, Heath's parents bought him lots of stuff because they could. Today, his dad is out of a job and has no discretionary money to buy anything that isn't a necessity. Heath is an angry, resentful teen, feeling entitled to luxuries he never learned to live without and now cannot afford.

THE PRINCIPLE
When we give them too much,
they don't learn the art of working and waiting.

This may be the worst attitude of all, and it tends to surface when we do too much for our children. They naturally begin acting entitled. They feel they deserve all the niceties and luxuries they see on television. These are really good kids deep down, but outsiders merely see their repulsive attitude of entitlement. They appear as...

lazy	ungrateful
jealous	discontent
impatient	undisciplined

The Generation iY Scene

In *Generation iY*, I describe teens who've grown up in the *i* world: iTunes, iPods, iPhones, iPads...you get the point. They've never known a day without the Internet. This is good news and bad news. Our world offers many conveniences and amenities our parents and grandparents never enjoyed. Thanks to technology and culture, the good news is, we obtain what we want faster and easier than ever before.

The bad news is, the *i* world presents us with new challenges to face with our kids. It shouldn't surprise us that the challenges of hard work and delayed gratification are greater today than in past generations. Just examine the world we created for Generation iY.

Their world is full of...	Consequently, they can assume...
Speed	Slow is bad.
Convenience	Hard is bad.
Entertainment	Boring is bad.
Nurture	Risk is bad.
Entitlement	Labor is bad.

Ironically, the things young people want to avoid are necessary for them to mature authentically. Slow, hard, boring, risky, laborious… these are the very challenges that prepare me to become a good man, a good husband, a good father, a good employee, a good employer. Many life skills that once naturally developed in us now atrophy in today's culture. So we must be far more intentional about leading our kids into opportunities to build these skills.

Moving from Helicopter to Lighthouse

When my daughter got her driver's license, she naturally wanted a car. Immediately. Unfortunately, she could not afford the car she wanted. In fact, she really couldn't afford any car when she turned 16. So she and I made a deal. We decided to split the cost of her first automobile. Whatever car she chose, she would have to pay for half of it. (This gave her incentive to keep the price reasonable.) She waited until she had a down payment, and we worked out a payment plan. Then, as she traded or sold her cars in the future, she would have at least some leverage as a down payment for the next one. This simple act helped prevent an attitude of entitlement and fostered gratitude when she finally got her used Ford Escape. My wife and I made sure it was a safe vehicle, and she made sure it was something she could maintain.

I didn't realize it at the time, but this single step kept me from being a helicopter parent and helped me to become a lighthouse parent. Let me illustrate what I mean.

Dan Tynan recently wrote about his son's first driver's license. Dan didn't want to distrust his son's skills or integrity, but he wanted to keep tabs on his safety, so he tried something new. He tracked his son's whereabouts with a GPS device.

> My son is an excellent driver, even if his foot has a little too much lead in it for my taste. It's the other crazy drivers that worry me. So this year, I deployed a secret weapon: the Audiovox Car Connection, a cigarette-lighter-sized device we plugged into the on-board diagnostics (OBD) port on our aging minivan.

The Car Connection can do a number of cool things. For example, it can tell you when it's time to rotate your tires or change your oil. It measures your car's fuel efficiency. It can tell you when the driver is traveling too fast or breaking too hard. If your kid has an Android or Blackberry phone, you can use it to block him from texting or talking while driving.

But mostly we wanted it for location tracking. Car Connection pings a GPS satellite every five minutes and displays its location on the Web…

Needless to say, my son was not entirely happy about this turn of events. "Why are you cyber-stalking me?" he grumbled.

Good question. And this is where the helicopter became a lighthouse. Dan and his wife sat down with their son and talked. Yep, they actually explained their leadership move and welcomed conversation.

My wife pointed out…if he drove the car into a ditch, banged his head, and forgot who we were or how to reach us, it would be nice to be able to locate him.

For a kid who drives with the tank perpetually empty— and who lives in terror of running out of gas and being stranded—this part resonated. "I guess that's OK then," he said, and went back to watching YouTube.[3]

Tynan adds, "Our motto, like the old US–Soviet negotiators: Trust, but verify." I love it.

Becoming a Lighthouse

This example shows how a potential helicopter parent chose to be a lighthouse parent instead, offering guidance but not hovering. Dan and his wife actually let their son (at age 16) go places independent of them, but they are giving him time to build trust until they no longer need the device.

A lighthouse is different from a helicopter. It doesn't move, but it's a beacon of light and communication. A lighthouse reveals location and provides guidance, but it won't chase you down. Check out the difference in a nutshell.

Helicopter Leader	Lighthouse Leader
hovers and controls	checks and communicates
is overactive, oversensitive	is a stable beacon to follow
follows kids around	won't chase kids down
tells kids how to behave	lets kids know where they stand
imposes rules and regulations	offers light and guidance

Let's Look at the Research

Robert Sun writes about the art of motivating students.

> Most people think raw intellectual talent is the primary marker for academic success among children. But new insights are proving that motivation is perhaps even more important to learning than innate intelligence.
>
> One widely cited study, recently published in the journal *Child Development,* supports the view that motivation and cognitive learning strategies outweigh intelligence as the top factors driving long-term achievement, particularly in math. Led by Kou Murayama...at the University of Munich, the study measured gains in math proficiency over a five-year period among 3,500 German students in grades five through ten. The study also asked the participants about their attitudes toward math.
>
> For the purposes of the study, Murayama and his team defined motivation as having three distinct components: intrinsic motivation, or the willingness to engage in a task

for its inherent pleasure and satisfaction; extrinsic motivation, driven by expected short-term benefits (e.g., good
grades); and perceived control, or the level of expectation
that one's efforts will produce a desired outcome...

Intrinsic motivation is propelled by emotion. Examine a
person's personal ambition to succeed and you will always
find an attitude or experience...that drives it. Children
need this "emotional fuel" to propel them towards mastery,
overcoming the many obstacles and setbacks they encounter along the way. Without emotional fuel, they easily give
up when the going gets rough.

Their fuel tank gets refilled each time a child puts out effort and
achieves something, internal or external.

Once they understand that they can achieve through effort,
they will keep trying. As they succeed in learning, they
find the joy and self-satisfaction that comes from mastering
new skills. The approach mirrors what Stanford University
psychologist Carol Dweck, in her landmark book *Mindset*,
says: that a growth mindset, rather than a fixed mindset, is
essential to personal development.[4]

We will discuss that more in chapter 10.

One takeaway from this research is clear. Simply giving something
to a child may make her happier in the moment, but not over time.
It actually reduces her strong sense of self. Self-esteem doesn't come
merely through affirmation. Research has demonstrated that affirmation without hard work fosters narcissism. Self-esteem is fostered by
effort and accomplishment. If kids are going to feel good about themselves, adults must balance unconditional love for children with allowing them to work hard and earn something. As kids grow up, they need
increased levels of autonomy ("I am free and can make decisions as I
perform") and responsibility ("I am accountable to follow through on
my commitment").

Cheating Them by Giving Them What They Should Earn

The mistake we're wrestling with in this chapter plays out in several contexts, not just in our homes. For instance, our current public school system has fallen prey to it. Teachers are my heroes, but the system we've created over time is faltering. Let me unveil one of my biggest concerns we face in education.

I mentioned it before. Today, students are cheating to get ahead. This may not be anything new, but they are cheating in larger numbers than any generation measured before them. They will cheat in elementary school for the challenge, they'll do it in middle school to get by, and they'll cheat in high school to get into their preferred college. Many students even admit to it. Our predisposition to give them things that we should require them to earn has fostered this attitude: Do whatever you have to do to get what you want.

The sad news is, a large number of states report a growing number of teachers who cheat as well. On March 7, 2011, *USA Today* ran a front-page article reporting teachers who adjusted test scores to make their school fare better when compared to schools in other districts, states, and nations. Results from states such as Arizona, California, Colorado, Florida, Michigan, and Ohio revealed a disparity between an entire class's performance one year and its performance the next. In the end, teachers began admitting to adjusting the scores.[5]

In a dangerous trend, we seem to be valuing the product more than the process. Instead of focusing on the art of learning to think well, we all just want to get the right score. Who cares if the kids learned how to solve problems or discovered how to think critically? We want to look good. We want to feel good as we compare our results to Japan or Denmark. We just want to get to the goal.

When I was a teenager, I ran long distance on the track team. One of my fellow runners and I were qualifying in a heat to run in the regional competition the following week. He decided to do something strange and illegal. Halfway through the race, he ducked behind the bleachers where no one could see him. He caught his breath, and on the last lap, he rejoined the race. He obviously won and qualified to compete in the regional championship. Can you guess what happened? He wasn't ready for the harsh competition. He vomited twice and dropped out.

Why? He'd cheated to get there. He was given what he did not earn. He valued the result more than the journey—the product more than the process. It always shows up in the end. This can ruin us unless we get back to the basics and teach our children and our students how to think regardless of their test scores. If we care about the future, our economy, the global competition they will face, and their readiness for adulthood, we will value the process.

Pause and reflect for a moment. As caring adults, we naturally want to provide for the young people around us, but there is such a thing as *overnurturing*. It happens when we give kids what they should earn. As I have argued, overnurturing ends up harming kids as they learn to depend on someone else and don't experience the intended satisfaction of accomplishing something for themselves. In other words, we can actually damage their sense of identity. What's more, we can disable them.

Let me illustrate. You may recall the story of wild pigs in the hills of West Virginia. No one could capture them. They ran wild for years until finally a nearby town offered a reward to anyone who could bring them in alive. A local farmer took up the challenge and began laying out huge amounts of food in the valleys in the area. When the sun set, the pigs smelled the food and sneaked in to devour it. Day after day, the man laid out a spread. He did this for months until he suspected the pigs had built a habit. Finally, one evening the man placed the food in the same place, but this time, he positioned a net around it. When the pigs came for their food, they were captured.

It was easy. They had gotten used to someone giving them what they should have been earning.

In one sense, they had become domesticated. The pigs were no longer using their skills or instincts to hunt for prey or to beware of the wild hills around them. Everyone loves a free lunch, right?

I'm not suggesting this story is a direct parallel, but it does illustrate a principle. Human beings operate in the same way. As I mentioned in chapter 4, statistics show that winning the lottery doesn't provide long-term wealth. Within a few years, the money is lost or spent, and life is back to normal. In fact, you're more likely to go bankrupt after winning the lottery than before. It's an illusion of wealth. Why? If you haven't learned to manage money before, having a lot of it only delays the inevitable. If we lived in a broken situation before, we tend to return to it afterward. I know it's a cliché, but it's true—give a man a fish, and he will eat for a day. Teach him how to fish, and he will eat for a lifetime.

The Unintended Consequences of Too Much Too Soon

Very often, we have to navigate new territory as we lead our kids. Perhaps our parents never modeled healthy leadership for us when we were growing up, and now we're emulating whatever leadership style we experienced as kids. Quite frequently, teachers and parents feel as if their kids' lifestyles are spinning out of control. The endless technology, the negative social connections, the content they're exposed to 24/7… it all leads us to want to impose some rules on them. After all, we know what's best for them. We default to seizing control. We make decisions for them. We provide for them. Often, we determine the course of their lives. We are large and in charge.

Consider, however, whether this is the best way to reach your desired outcome.

Generally speaking, we believe that more is better, faster is better, sooner is better. We want to provide more for our children, and we want to do it right away—for the improvement of our society, of course.

So we continue to push children to learn more, faster. Parents are placing kids in school at three years old, not five or six. We want to get the learning process started earlier so they can get a jump on their peers as adolescents. It makes sense.

But we fail to recognize that even though their brain may be able to consume data earlier, the rest of their soul (their will and their emotions) may not be ready for it. When parents pause to actually think about it, they agree. According to a *USA Today* survey, nearly six in ten moms say children are growing up too fast. By this, they mean we are exposing them to realities before they're emotionally ready. The survey reported these statistics:

- 75 percent say parents allow Internet use without supervision too soon.
- 74 percent say parents dress their kids in age-inappropriate clothing.
- 63 percent say parents overschedule their kids' lives.
- 59 percent say parents give kids cell phones too early.[6]

In this overexposed, pressurized lifestyle, kids become overwhelmed. We all do. In response, we compensate by giving kids things to lessen the pressure. In other words, amid the stress, we often make decisions to soften the experience, giving kids what they should earn. It's one of many symptoms of reactionary leadership. Overwhelmed lives lead us to react. We throw money at problems, we bend the rules, we patch things up rather than make things right, we give in to demands...and we give our kids things.

It's no wonder college graduates return home feeling unready for the real world. They often aren't. Their life skills and emotional intelligence are low. Their sense of direction is low. By their twenties, they become a postponed generation—delaying adult responsibility instead of embracing it.

The *Los Angeles Times* reported the results of two national surveys by Nickelodeon and the market research firm Harris Interactive. The reports state that more than three out of four kids said they are not in any hurry to grow up. When I was a kid, we could hardly wait to grow up. Today, kids want to stay right where they are.

The findings startle many childhood researchers, who've watched as today's kids cast off dolls earlier and gravitate to all things teenage. Yet the phenomenon seems to echo a shift already spotted among teens and twentysomethings—the lengthening road into adulthood. Kids are growing up too fast and too slow at the same time. Nickelodeon chalks up the change among kids to the forces of helicopter parents who don't prepare them.[7]

The Value of Work

May I suggest one remedy for the problem of giving them what they should be earning? I have believed for years that work is a key element in kids' maturation. There is a definite correlation between working—being productive—and maturity. I got my first job at 12, tossing newspapers on driveways for less than minimum wage. I did it before school, so it was dark and often rainy as I packed my papers on my bike each day. At 16, I got my first real job, working at a fast-food restaurant. Before I had a car, I rode my bike four miles to work and four miles back after my shift. In college, I worked three jobs while carrying a full load of classes. At the time, I did it because I needed the money. I had no idea how it was building my character, improving my work ethic, and cultivating my appreciation for everyday blessings and benefits. Like vegetables, work was good for me.

Today, most teens in America are not employed. They don't have to be. For some reason, Mom and Dad have decided it's better for them to play a sport, dance, or sing. I appreciate all those things, but they are virtual experiences. Unless the kid becomes a professional at those activities, they are facsimiles of real life. Students can learn discipline from them, but these experiences do not trade value for value as work does.

Work Versus Other After-School Activities

Why have we chosen to enroll our kids in after-school activities rather than encourage them to enter the workforce? Here are four reasons.

- Mom and Dad can afford to give their kids spending money for almost everything, and they believe that's what good parents do. Ten years ago, the US Department of Labor reported that the average teen had $87 a week to spend.

- Society feels that a job forces a child to grow up too quickly. We see kids being pushed into increasingly stressful regimens—more school hours, homework, testing, and performances—and we fear they have to grow up too fast. Not working is one way to continue being a kid.

- When our kids play a sport or an instrument, they stay under our general supervision. At work, they do not. We are obsessed with safety in America, and we feel work may not be safe. And quite frankly, we like to be in control. We can be control freaks.

- Work is generally perceived as boring, and *boring* is almost a cussword. Ask average teens what they hate most—being bored will likely make their top-five list. Other activities aren't as productive, but they keep our kids entertained.

May I toss a thought into the ring? Work shapes us. Being productive is innately good for human beings. This is one reason why so many unemployed people struggle to become the best version of themselves. Work enables us to express ourselves in exchange for money, to identify and groom our talents, and to cultivate healthy self-esteem because we are adding value to others. From a purely spiritual standpoint, it is a divine gift. Work can be an act of worship to our Creator.

It's no wonder American kids are finding it hard to grow up, no wonder the average teen delays acquiring a driver's license one full year, no wonder teens feel entitled to things they haven't earned. They often don't even do chores around the house. Adults do. And often, adults understand the value of work. Don't you think perhaps we've done our kids a disservice?

The largest unemployed demographic in the United States continues to be young adults aged 16 to 29. The reason is not merely a bad economy, although that hasn't helped. For many, jobs are readily available. Sadly, teens feel that the jobs that are available are beneath them. (In recent focus groups, adolescents told me that yard work or working in a fast-food restaurant is below them.) A century ago, four-year-old kids did age-appropriate chores around the house. It was normal, and it enabled them to mature in a healthy way.

Let me suggest some fundamental benefits that work offers us. When we labor at something meaningful—offering goods or services to our community—we earn much more than money.

Good work helps us identify our gifts.

When we get a job, we can experiment with tasks that can confirm where our greatest gifts and talents lie. The closer we get to serving in our sweet spot, the deeper our sense of satisfaction.

Good work helps us develop discipline.

When we're on the job, our only motivation may be to get the next paycheck. But along the way, we deepen our disciplines. We hone our ability to delay gratification and get beyond doing only what feels good.

Good work raises our self-esteem.

Working a job typically cultivates our self-image. We gain a deeper sense of pride about ourselves, a greater sense of dignity. We want to live by a higher standard. As one proverb says, "He that hates discipline despises himself."

Good work provides big-picture vision.

When we work, we tend to gain perspective. We can see beyond ourselves; we are humbled by it. We learn that activities we assumed were easy really aren't. We appreciate money and what it buys because we know how many hours we spent earning it.

Good work furnishes fulfillment.

Finally, when we work at something we believe in, the reward can be internal. More than a salary, we gain an inward sense of gratification. We've added value; we can step back and look with satisfaction at what we've accomplished. This is a divine gift.

If the young people in your care "just aren't into working," may I suggest you talk over these five benefits with them? Perhaps they've never seen adults work at jobs they love. Or they've never seen a job they felt actually mattered. Let's model laboring at something that counts—and enjoying it. In this way, kids can "learn to earn" instead of feeling entitled to things.

Doing the Hard Thing

Putting our kids to work in age-appropriate ways will likely be difficult. They may tell you what you've asked them to do is too hard (this is the number one comment K-12 teachers tell me students say to them in class). For the sake of their own growth, you are taking a hard stand. You're not merely giving them something, but enabling them to work for it.

Here's a case in point. My friend Eddie has three kids, ages 16, 14, and 12. After reading my blog posts on this subject, he decided summertime would look different around their house. He made up a flyer to be passed around the neighborhood. It let folks know that he and his kids were available to mow lawns, rake leaves, trim hedges, clean up, and paint. Before heading to the pool, his kids placed flyers on their neighbors' front doors. Reluctantly, at first. They rolled their eyes in disbelief in the beginning. And then the phone began to ring.

When Eddie told me this story, the summer had dramatically changed his kids. He told me how they were actually getting to know the adults on their street. He said they learned how to respond to different kinds of bosses—some of the neighbors stood over the kids as they picked up the leaves, and others trusted them to do it on their own. They learned respect. He even said that during video games, his kids would stop early, saying they had to go finish a job down the street. He was amazed at how responsible his kids were with the tasks and how grateful they were for the money they'd earned.

Another case in point. A new experiment at a high school in New Haven, Connecticut, ended the year with shocking results: Not a single one of the 44 first-time freshmen earned enough credits to become a sophomore.

Teachers, newly empowered to break from traditional practices, have begun to reinvent the high school experience by switching freshmen to a self-paced system where kids move up only when they've "mastered" specific skills. The goal is to make sure kids learn something instead of breezing through school with Ds…

Unlike at other schools, these 44 kids won't have to repeat freshman year. They'll get an opportunity to finish their work over a new, four-week summer school…Then, if they need more time, they can start off the year right where they left off instead of repeating entire classes.[8]

The key is, they have to earn their progress.

Six Steps to Bring Out the Best in Our Kids

Please understand, I'm not suggesting if you've made this mistake—giving kids what they should earn—that you suddenly demand a transformation. That kind of abrupt shift could backfire. I do believe, however, that we need to introduce them to change. So how do we help these kids become all they could be at home and at school? How do we build a bridge from the coddled life to the disciplined life that adulthood will demand? From our student focus groups, I've discovered six steps parents and teachers can take.

Cultivate a relationship.

Every student panel and focus group we host asks for this. Kids wish their parents, coaches, or teachers would actually pursue some kind of relationship with them. Often students are reticent to initiate this. They question whether adults will welcome a relationship. To be honest, we often don't. We're tired and busy. Why not approach kids, start conversations, ask personal questions, and let them know you care?

Earn the right to be heard.

I know you're the leader, but this generation of kids has not been taught to respect the badge or the title. You may have authority, but you must earn your influence. Build trust by doing what you say you'll do. Show up on time if you require punctuality from students. Embody the attitude you demand of them.

Often, the best way to earn the right to be heard is to listen.

Communicate belief.

You can't fake this. Teachers and coaches who win their students over, authentically communicate that they believe in them. The same goes for parents. In fact, make the effort to convince them that you are pushing them because you believe they have potential to succeed. Every young man and woman needs a caring adult to look them in the eye and say, "I believe you have it in you. I'm convinced you have what it takes to succeed."

Teach and lead like a mentor.

All of our student focus groups express how much they want their teachers to be mentors. They actually expect their parents to be mentors. This requires a connection beyond lectures and grades. When mentors teach, they do it in the spirit of hope, desiring their students to grasp the concepts, apply them, and ultimately win. Once again, this requires relationship, belief, motivation, and passion for the students.

Remove the fear of failure.

Often kids don't try because they've been conditioned to think failure is unacceptable. Many of them have never failed or struggled—they have ribbons and trophies in their rooms just for playing. But now, failure is an option, and they don't want to let anyone down, so they don't try. Adults must clearly relay to them that failure isn't final or fatal. In fact, it's the way everyone really learns and grows.

Challenge them with a hard assignment.

I have come to believe that deep down, every kid wants to be involved with a project that's important and almost impossible. When we give a tough assignment (at home or at school) and let them know it will take everything they've got, we're communicating that we actually take them seriously. They are legit. On a foundation of support and belief, this is a logical way to prove you think they can really do it.

One last thought. This may take time. We really do need to build a bridge they can cross from artificial maturity to authentic maturity. For years, parents may have made kids the center of their lives, so change won't happen overnight. I believe, however, if we'll follow these steps, we can help kids grow up into great adults over time.

My friend David has a son named Nick. Years ago when Nick was in middle school, he told his dad about a new iPod that just came out. He wanted it badly and convinced his dad that they would sell out quickly. David asked his son if he had enough money to buy it. Nick looked down and mumbled that he didn't. Then, looking up hopefully, he asked Dad if he'd buy it for him.

David was in a quandary. He loves his kids just as you love yours. At the same time, he knew that simply buying it for Nick wasn't the best way to lead him in that moment. He didn't want to foster immediate gratification in his oldest son. So David responded in a very wise way.

"Nick, I'm going to buy that new iPod so we won't miss out if they sell out. However, because I'm buying it, it's mine for now. I am going to allow you to make whatever payments you can each week or each month until you pay it off (at no interest). Once you pay for it, I will give it to you. I know you can do this."

Nick smiled and agreed.

David told me that a few months later, Nick made his final payment and got the iPod from his dad. He also told me how much Nick had learned gratitude, discipline, and patience in the process.

We Praise the Wrong Things

Brianna's story is like so many others but perhaps more tragic.

As a young girl, she was acutely aware of how her parents complimented other girls on their beauty. They would say, "I love your shiny hair," and "Your dress looks so pretty today," and "You've got the prettiest eyes of anyone in your class."

As Brianna heard her parents affirm other kids' looks, she began working hard to look good herself. She desperately wanted to be the apple of her parents' eye. As her mom and dad complimented her, she began a silent competition with other girls. She wanted to hear more about her beautiful looks than anyone else's. And then the inevitable happened.

As she matured, she began to feel she wasn't pretty. In fact, she decided she was fat. As a young teen, she endured her worst years. She struggled with bulimia. This led to traumatic freshman and sophomore years of high school. She fought battles with acne, her weight, her height, and her self-esteem.

The good news is, she came through it. By her junior year, she determined she was no homecoming queen, so she decided to focus on her studies. Her parents began telling her she was smart. At this point, a whole new addiction surfaced. She became dependent on affirmation about her intelligence. After all, kids tend to play the game they figure they can win. But the encouragement could not come in fast enough.

I spoke to Brianna recently. She's now 28 but remains a fragile woman, still in need of affirmation from others. Her identity continues to be insecure—she still doesn't believe she's pretty or smart.

Addicted to Praise

Everyone agrees that kids need encouragement. In fact, we all need it. Encouragement is oxygen for the soul. Desiring our kids to have every advantage possible, we want them to get plenty of encouragement. This is why so many of us have lavished our kids with praise, complimenting their every move and affirming every trait imaginable. This has been a gigantic shift from past generations of parents and kids, where praise was rare and kids weren't the center of their families. The pendulum has swung far to the other side, and we haven't recognized how it's impacted our culture. The affirmation of children has become a controversial subject today.

Praise and affirmation have become so prevalent, they have lost their true value. Telling our teens, "You're awesome!" or "You're the best singer [or pitcher or quarterback] in the world!" has diminished the strength of our words. It's supply and demand. With such a large supply, the demand has decreased. Affirmation means less than it once did.

In addition to turning up the volume of our praise, we've become a bit careless with the content. Without thinking, we make reckless, flattering remarks that feel good in the moment but that may steer kids in the wrong direction. That flattery is likely focused on their smarts or looks or talent—and can actually do more harm than good.

What gets rewarded gets repeated.

When we affirm looks or clothing—external matters instead of internal virtues—kids' values become skewed. Remember, what gets rewarded gets repeated. Without realizing it, we are reinforcing cosmetic features—usually features that are not in their control. Adults often continue to fall into the trap of praising fixed qualities, thinking we should associate desirable traits with their identity.

You're smart.
You're beautiful.
You're gifted.
You're sharp.

We should be doing just the opposite. We must affirm effort and behavior, which are in their control, instead of characteristics that are out of their control. If we do this, we begin to foster a growth mindset instead of a fixed mindset. Affirming that they're smart (fixed mindset) fosters the thought, "I'm intelligent. It's who I am, so I shouldn't have to try hard."

According to a survey conducted by Columbia University, 85 percent of American parents think it's important to tell their kids that they're smart. We all seem to do it. We feel saying these words will somehow help them enter their next school exam with a little more confidence. It just seems to roll off our tongues. Parents in our focus groups typically brag about how much they praise their children. They claim to do it early, often, and with no plans to stop.

> At pick up one recent afternoon, parents at a Burbank preschool received a cautionary note. It wasn't a notice about lice or eating too much sugar. Instead, parents were advised against constantly telling their toddlers "good job!" and offered other suggestions on how to encourage them.
>
> The newsletter admonishment shows that research into the negative effects of too much praise is now fairly well-known and accepted—at least by early childhood experts. It also shows, however, that parents aren't really listening.[1]

We keep doing it in spite of what the childhood experts say. "This is precisely the problem with praise, or at least praise aimed at performance," writes Jenny Anderson, from the *New York Times*. "It's like crack for kids: Once they get it, they need it, and they want more. And the real world doesn't praise them for getting dressed in the morning."[2]

We have found that praise has backfired for so many kids.

──────────── **THE PRINCIPLE** ────────────

When we affirm looks or smarts instead of virtues,
their values can become skewed.

I received a letter from a parent in response to a blog post on this topic. Within four months, the blog had been shared more than a million times. (It actually inspired this book.) The mom wrote a thank-you but shared her tragic story along the way.

Dear Tim,

I read your article "Three Huge Mistakes We Make Leading Kids," and it brought me to tears. Our oldest son would be 22 years old today. He excelled in school, and somewhere along the way his teachers and grandparents started calling him gifted and a genius. As much as we didn't like the terms, my husband and I went along because we wanted our son to have good self-esteem. During his junior year of college our son started having a hard time in a statistics class. He frequently complained about the tediousness of the problems and the amount of homework.

Tragically, our son committed suicide after taking his finals. We don't know why; we will never know why. In reflecting on his life, my husband and I now realize that during high school our son was unable to accept failure and hid his failures at all costs. During high school, he would only bring home the graded papers with As. He didn't know how to handle anything less than an A and certainly did not want to discuss lesser grades. He did get a few Bs on his report card, which were devastating. We look back to the early grammar school years and equate all the praise given for good grades to giving a child a bag full of sugar candy. Our son was on a sugar high from the praise. None of us had any idea.

I now subscribe to your blogs. We have three younger kids and I've been reading all I can to try to figure out where we went wrong and how to do this differently. Thank you for your article. It has already helped.

Sincerely,
Linda

Misguided Praise

Jenn Berman, a marriage and family therapist and author, agrees. "We are becoming praise junkies as parents. We've gone to the opposite extreme of a few decades ago, when parents tended to be more strict. And now we over-praise our children."[3] Last year, I attended a conference where I discovered HR departments in companies could not keep up with the need for feedback and affirmation from their young employees. In response, they've hired "praise consultants" who provide the needed compliments. This HR challenge points to a praise problem.

Here are the three most common praise mistakes I see.

We praise fixed features.

Saying to our kids, "You're smart," or "You're pretty," or "You're gifted," seems like the perfect way to affirm their identity. It is, in fact, precisely the way to ruin them. It is far better to affirm effort or virtues they can choose to practice. More on this later.

We praise carelessly.

I see many parents praise their kids without thinking. Kids are told they're amazing when they draw a picture, win a ballgame, get a decent grade, pour a drink without spilling it, or some other ordinary activity. Parents think that by giving kids heaping portions of praise, they're building their children's confidence and sense of self, when in fact they may be doing just the opposite. They may be reducing it. Careless praise becomes hollow and means little over time.

Our praise doesn't match their performance.

We live in a world of hyperbole. We think we must exaggerate to be heard. So we use words like *awesome* or *excellent* when our kids have done merely what is expected of them. We offer huge praise for minimal effort. As our children grow older, matching the affirmation with the effort becomes especially important. Not too little, but not too much. This is how trust is built, and it's why kids continue to listen to their parents during their teen years.

"Somehow, parents have come to believe that by praising their kids they improve their self-esteem," Paul Donahue, founder and director of Child Development Associates, says. "Though well-intentioned, putting kids on a pedestal at an early age can actually hinder their growth."[4]

Let me list a handful of reasons this can happen.

Praise can diminish motivation.

As I will explain later, researchers at Columbia University found that when kids were praised for their intellect instead of their hard work, they tended to lose motivation if they performed poorly on a test or project. These children operated under the misguided assumption that they did well only because they were smart, not because they studied or worked hard. When we praise our children for inherent traits over which they have no control, such as beauty, intelligence, or athleticism, they'll assume they shouldn't have to try hard. What's more, sooner or later, these traits might fade.

It can increase narcissism.

Research on the self-esteem movement has turned up some interesting discoveries. Dr. Roy Baumeister, a leading advocate of self-esteem research, has admitted the data is the biggest disappointment of his career. He concluded that self-esteem does not improve grades, advance careers, or lower violence. He now concludes that praise for college students actually causes grades to sink. Sadly, we've learned that constant affirmation creates narcissism, not self-esteem. We begin cultivating kids who are preoccupied with themselves instead of secure enough to look outward and empathize with others.

It can create insecurity.

Parents often assume that consistent praise will build a child's self-esteem, but sometimes the opposite is true. True self-esteem is an internal quality that comes from mastering difficult tasks and making meaningful contributions. A child's inner sense of pride for a job well done means more than any kudos from an external source.

If you constantly praise your child, she might come to need and expect your approval, rather than learning to gauge success for herself, according to the University of Minnesota Extension office. Children who are addicted to praise become insecure and anxious if they don't receive accolades for every positive success.[5]

It can displace focus.

When children are constantly rewarded for their efforts, they might come to view the reward as more important than the experience. Stickers, reward charts, merit badges, and other common rewards replace the intrinsic value of an experience. In fact, the 2006 Brown Report on Education from the Brookings Institution found that children from countries in which educators and parents focus on self-esteem have lower academic achievement than when the focus is on effort and results. Think twice before rewarding, and focus on the satisfaction of the activity. To encourage a love of reading, for example, read engaging fiction together or use books to learn a new skill. Model a love of reading yourself.[6]

It can confuse identity.

The truth is, with truckloads of praise, kids have a hard time distinguishing what fits them and what doesn't. As they grow older, they often realize Mom is the only one telling them they are awesome, and they begin to question her judgment. Further, teenagers believe that teachers praise the ones who need praise—it's not a sign you did well, but that you lack ability. They recognize the psychology of it all. Further, if kids have been told they're smart, for instance, they tend to compare themselves to others rather than prepare for the next test. They get consumed with their ranking.[7]

In my book *Generation iY*, I share Laura's story. Laura told me that although she'd written a bestseller, she felt like a fraud, as if she really hadn't lived up to her potential. She dismissed her achievements as not good enough because they paled against her supposedly spectacular promise. Nothing was good enough. She said she was not only failing to write any good books, she stopped writing books at all. She knew she needed help.

As I spoke to Laura, I felt someone was finally talking honestly with me about childhood dilemmas we sweep under the rug today. She mentioned when she arrived at college, she got her first glimmer that her future might not be as brilliant as she had expected. She was shocked to find there were hordes of gifted kids just like her. They, too, had heard from parents and teachers that they were special, that they were going to the top of the heap. Laura was now in the middle of that heap.

Laura went on, sharing the wisdom she'd gleaned over the years. Early aptitude doesn't necessarily predict adult accomplishment. In fact, the opposite may be truer. Author Malcolm Gladwell, in his speech "American Obsession with Precociousness," pointed out that few childhood prodigies ever become successful. That's because there's a huge difference between talent and the application of talent...if everyone tells you when you're 10 that you'll become a great journalist, you just sit back and dream about your book jackets. Not only don't precocious kids think they have to work hard, but deep down, they believe true effort entails too much risk."

Think about it. When children hear they are destined to be great, the thought that they might produce something mediocre is devastating. It's too risky to even try. Even giving a good performance isn't satisfying. They feel the pressure to be the best...or forget it.

The Research: When Praising Our Kids Backfires

I mentioned earlier, 85 percent of parents today think it's important to tell their kids they are smart. The assumption is that if a student believes he's smart (having been affirmed so repeatedly), he won't be intimidated by new academic challenges. The constant praise is meant to be an angel on their shoulder, reminding them how great they are.

But a growing body of research is showing us today this practice is backfiring. Dr. Carol Dweck, author of *Mindset*, led a team of researchers in New York public schools and discovered what many of us knew intuitively. Dweck sent her research assistants into fifth-grade classes to give them puzzles to do. Once students finished the tests, they were randomly divided into groups and told their score. Then half of them were told, "You must be smart." The other half were told, "You must have really worked hard."

Next, the students were given a choice for a second test. They were told they could choose a more difficult test that would teach them a lot, or they could choose an easy test, just like the first one. Of the students praised for their effort, 90 percent chose the harder test. Of those praised for their intelligence, the vast majority chose the easy test. The "smart" kids took the cop-out.

When questioned why this happened, Dr. Dweck was clear on her conclusion. "When we praise students for their intelligence, we teach them this is the name of the game: Look smart. Don't risk making mistakes." And that's what the kids had done. They'd chosen to look smart and avoid the risk of being embarrassed. The students who took the harder test (one designed for seventh graders) all failed. But Dweck reported they could see they were positively challenged by it. In fact, several kids remarked as they took the exam, "This is my favorite test."

Finally, the researchers gave the students one last test designed to be as easy as the first one. Dweck suspected the kids that were praised for being smart might struggle a bit but had no idea how much they would. Those who'd been praised for their effort improved significantly on the third test—by about 30 percent. Those who'd been told they were smart did worse than they had on the first test—by about 20 percent.

Dweck's team now concludes that when we praise kids for their effort, we give them a variable they can control. When we simply tell kids they're smart, we teach them they have innate intelligence and they think they don't have to work hard. In fact, they begin to fear they may fail to confirm the adults who believe they're smart, and they don't want to try anything in which they may fail.[8]

How Does This Affect Their Relationship with You?

Studies consistently link self-esteem and happiness. Our children can't have one without the other. It's something we know intuitively, and it turns many of us into overzealous cheerleaders. Our child scribbles and we declare him a Picasso, scores a goal and he's the next Beckham, adds 1 and 2 and he's ready for Mensa. But this sort of "achievement praise" can backfire.

"The danger, if this is the only kind of praise a child hears, is that he'll think he needs to achieve to win your approval," [author Bob] Murray explains. "He'll become afraid that if he doesn't succeed, he'll fall off the pedestal and his parents won't love him anymore." Praising specific traits—intelligence, prettiness, athleticism—can also undermine children's confidence later, if they grow up believing they're valued for something that's out of their control and potentially fleeting.

"If you praise your child primarily for being pretty, for example, what happens when she grows old and loses that beauty?" Murray asks. "How many facials will it take for her to feel worthwhile?" Interestingly, Murray adds, research shows that kids who are praised mainly for being bright become intellectually timid, fearing that they will be seen as less smart—and less valuable—if they fail.

The antidote, however, is not to withhold praise but rather to redirect it, Murray says. "Praise the effort rather than the result," he advises. "Praise the creativity, the hard work, the persistence, that goes into achieving, more than the achievement itself."[9]

So, what is the right amount of praise? Research indicates that the quality of praise is more important than the quantity. If praise is sincere and genuine and focused on the effort, not the outcome, you can give it as often as your children do something that warrants a verbal reward. Just keep an eye on how it impacts your kids over time.

Let's Appraise Our Praise

In light of this research, what are some changes to make as we seek to affirm kids? Are there solutions to better direct students into healthy and responsible maturity? Yes there are!

1. Praise them for effort, not for their intelligence or beauty.

2. Reward character virtues (such as honesty) more than performance—early on.

3. Teach them to enjoy the process (the journey) as much as the product.

4. Make sure the size and content of your praise matches their effort.

5. Be sure your affirmation is sincere, thoughtful, and genuine.

6. Empower them by helping them own a personal set of values to live by.

7. Identify and affirm unique features that differentiate your kids.

8. Provide experiences for them to discover and build their primary strengths.

9. Furnish a platform for them to serve others using their strengths and gifts.

10. Tell them you enjoy watching them perform regardless of the outcome.

11. The younger they are, the more immediate your feedback for them must be.

12. Equip them to take risks and learn that failure is okay as long as they tried.

13. Build a secure home for them but one that does not revolve around them.

14. When in doubt, always praise what is in their control.

15. Clarify your unconditional love for them regardless of their performance.

My friend Andy Lorenzen has practiced principles like these with his children for years. I enjoy talking with him about how well-adjusted his kids are because he and his wife have chosen to be intentional about their encouragement and praise. Andy will readily admit it's easy to succumb to parenting temptations, such as rescuing his kids from hardship or communicating over-the-top praise when they perform well. But his wise parenting is producing healthy kids who value character and are ready for the world that awaits them when they leave home one day.

It's What's Inside That Counts

Recently, I heard about a young boy named Conner.

Conner was born on April 7, 2000, a bit different than most. He suffered from bilateral Proximal Femoral Focal Deficiency (PFFD), a birth defect that caused him to be born without hips, ankles, femurs or knees. Essentially he only had his tibia and feet from the waist down. Of the few affected by this rare condition, only 15 percent have both legs affected like Conner.

By age two Conner's parents, Rita and Dewey Stroud, decided after consulting with doctors it would be best to have his two feet removed. Born with no ankles, there was little Conner could do with his feet. He underwent a half-amputee surgery in which doctors removed the front half of his feet, leaving only his heels.

The decision to perform the surgery was one of the most difficult the Strouds have ever had to make. As Rita explained, the doctors were unsure whether he'd ever be able to walk again and believed he would likely be restricted to a wheelchair for the remainder of his life. Fortunately for the Stroud family, Conner's resilience is unlike anything they've ever witnessed…

Conner began playing tennis when he was four years old. His mother ardently tried to persuade him to play wheelchair tennis, thinking it would be easier for him to be competitive. He quickly proved her wrong.

"When he was younger I never thought he would play tournaments like he has, I always thought maybe someday he'd just play wheelchair tennis," Rita said. "But he was so driven to play and compete in tournaments. I was concerned it would be too hard for him at first. Obviously you don't want your kid to struggle and I wasn't sure if he'd be able to compete. Winning isn't everything, but I wasn't sure he'd even be able to win a point."

After years of perfecting his own swing, Conner began to play in 8 and Under tournaments. It didn't take long for him to experience success. He won his very first tournament playing doubles with a friend. In his next tournament, he played singles for the first time. He won that tournament, too. Winning, however, didn't come without hard work and training. Because he was born without hips, it is very difficult for him to perform basic moves like turning sideways. With his lateral movement compromised, he's had to make some unique adjustments…

During his eight years of playing, Conner has encountered many challenges. But contrary to what one might believe, it's not his physical attributes that have been his toughest obstacles, it's the mental game.

"The most frustrating thing is being unable to get to the ball when people hit it away from me," Conner said. "All I can do is try to stay positive and not let it get to me."

It's the battle within that Rita believes has molded her son into such a strong person and inspiration to many.[10]

And this is the department where Conner's parents have been stellar. Each step of the way, they have affirmed Conner's ambition, yet they've praised his effort, not the wins. They've focused on what he has inside, not what he lacks on the outside. They've affirmed the process, not the trophy at the end. They have cried and celebrated together along the way, and this has made Conner durable. He hasn't let his struggles hinder his attitude, which is why he became such a sensation around the tennis community. People of all ages gravitate toward him.

> "He always draws a crowd," Rita said. "That's why he's such a good sport, because he knows I'll get on him if he acts up. People don't remember the best player at the tournament, they remember him. He's so fun to watch because he is so small and people are just amazed by his skills and the way he handles himself."[11]

Dealing with Change

It's the growth factor, over time, that's made life interesting for Conner.

> Despite his success on the court at an early age, Conner realizes his stretch of playing "normal tennis" is coming to an end. As players continue to mature at his age level, he's noticed his short legs will only allow him to do so much…

> Conner and his family attended a national wheelchair tournament in Hilton Head, SC, where he was able to talk to the athletes and pick up some pointers. Although adjusting to wheelchair tennis is no easy task, Conner said he's up to the challenge.

> "It's been really difficult to learn to steer and swing at the same time," Conner said. "But I've got pretty used to it playing against my dad, who bought a wheelchair of his

own to play alongside me. In fact, I'm even beating him now"...

Today, Conner's friends and family don't even look at him as handicapped. He radiates confidence and moves around like everyone else—he's just a bit shorter.

"He's just so strong and handles his situation very well," Rita said. "Kids are always following him around, staring and asking questions. He just takes it all in stride. In fact, he often jokes with people about what happened to him."[12]

What enables him to do this? Parents who've handled the art of praise and encouragement very well. They've never glossed over the challenges Conner will face, but they've enabled him to laugh, hope, and work hard through it all.

Now, *that's* what I call a well-adjusted kid.

We Value Removing All Pain

When our son was seven years old, he went through a challenging stage of life. I'd come home from work, and my wife would tell me he'd been bouncing off the walls all day. His energy was high, but his self-regulation was low. He was loud in restaurants and stores. He was always moving and frequently got into trouble. Once he almost gouged his eye out climbing on a clothes rack at a department store. We were in an emergency room within minutes, holding him down on a bed while a doctor attempted to repair the damage. After a year of this stage, we were almost at the end of our rope.

As my wife and I discussed getting Jonathan diagnosed for ADHD or some other condition, we paused and asked ourselves an important question—Did we want to put him on meds to reduce *his* pain or to reduce *our* pain?

I believe the first issue we parents must deal with is our own selfishness. We love our kids, but often we choose the path of ease and simplicity over the challenge of training them to become healthy adults. Fixing problems superficially is quicker and easier than equipping our kids to go the distance. Sometimes it is a painful process—for them and for us.

We chose to make one more attempt at resolving the situation without the use of medication. I'm not against medication—I need it each and every day as a diabetic—but I knew I didn't want Jonathan to immediately jump into using a prescription that had the potential to become addictive. If there was any way to solve the problem naturally through specific direction and healthy boundaries for our son, that would be our first course of action.

So we worked with Jonathan consistently on his behavior and attitudes. We gave him clear direction on his "inside" and "outside" voices. He knew the benefits and consequences of specific behaviors. We generously praised his effort, and like clockwork, we gave him places where he could cut loose and be a rambunctious boy. Sometimes we were in tears because of the excruciating effort required to consistently discipline him and to follow through on the consequences of his inappropriate conduct. Yet there were days the progress was unmistakable.

It took months, but our efforts paid off. The experience was painful but very rewarding. And now, having passed through that era of his childhood, we have learned an important lesson of childhood and parenting: The removal of pain is not the endgame.

Pause and reflect with me for a moment. We live in a time when we naturally and intuitively believe that removing pain is what good parents do. After all, we love our kids, and love requires us to comfort them. The implication is that we must take away any discomfort that intrudes into their lives. So we go on a warpath to keep them safe, medicate any aches or ailments, give them soft and safe places to scream or vent, and prevent any pain from interfering with their lives. We lock the door, put pads and helmets on them, and tell them never to touch a sharp tool.

But is that really a good approach over the long haul?

I don't think so. In fact, after raising both of our kids, I've come to believe if I really love them, I need to collaborate with them to help them navigate their way through the pain instead of always removing it. I've determined I must enable them to deal with the pain that accompanies life while encouraging them to remain grateful and content. My goal was to teach them that pleasure is not the removal of pain, but the satisfaction that comes when they overcome it as they pursue their life's purpose. This enables them to become sturdy, assured of my love, and equipped to stand strong in painful moments.

When our daughter, Bethany, was in middle school, her school hosted a dance. I'm sure you're aware that middle school is one of the most difficult periods of childhood. As hormones rage, kids are figuring out their identity and jockeying for popularity. Social status is everything.

Our daughter has become a beautiful young woman, but her middle school years were like many girls'. She didn't look like a Barbie doll. So she waited and waited for a boy to call and ask her to the dance. No one was calling her. Soon, my wife and I began hearing about other parents of middle school girls stepping in to control the situation. They were calling their friends and requesting that their sons ask their little girls to the dance. They gave suggestions on where to eat and what flowers to buy her. They even offered to fund the evening.

We considered this move. It certainly would have ended the painful waiting period and might have boosted Bethany's self-esteem. I'm certain that's why these other parents stepped in to seize control. On the other hand, we knew this might be a perfect time for her to learn how to navigate such a painful situation. We had several conversations with her, and we took a few walks down memory lane, reminiscing about dances in our day. Then we suggested that perhaps she could go Dutch with a group of friends. She eventually grew satisfied with that solution. Her contentment level was back to normal. And in the end, a friend did ask her to the dance—at the last minute. (Ugh—middle school boys!)

This was a crucial period for my wife and me. We are part of a generation that believes in removing pain from our children's lives. We have a pill for everything. We want them to have a better life than we had. Yet we faced vital questions: Is a better life one that has less pain but fails to prepare them for pain in adulthood? Or is it one that teaches them to navigate pain during a relatively safe period of their lives? We chose the latter.

Our Disdain for Pain

This requires intentional effort. Correcting this mistake is counterintuitive. As parents, we seem to have this natural inclination to remove pain. Edwin Bliss offers this reminder:

We live in a culture that worships comfort. During the last century, we have seen the greatest assault on discomfort in the history of the human race. We have learned to control our environment with central heating and air conditioning; we have reduced drudgery with machines and computers; we have learned to control pain, depression and stress; we even provide electronic antidotes to boredom with televisions sets and video games.

Most of this is good, but unfortunately it's created an impression that the purpose of life is to attain a blissful state of nirvana, a total absence of struggle or pain. The emphasis is on consuming, not producing; on short-term hedonism rather than long-term satisfaction. We seek immediate gratification of our desires with no penalties.

Life really doesn't work that way—at least not for many and not for long. One of Benjamin Franklin's favorite sayings was, "There's no gain without pain." And it's as true today as it was when it first appeared in Poor Richard's Almanac. The great goal of becoming what one is capable of becoming can be achieved only by those willing to pay the price, and the price always involves sacrifice, discomfort, unpleasantness, and yes, even pain.[1]

The Big Four

These are generally our big four parental pain-removing tactics:

- We *medicate*… giving kids an aid to eliminate aches. We offer an external painkiller so they don't feel badly.

- We *initiate*… stepping in to intervene on their behalf. Before they have a chance to solve their problem, we solve it for them.

- We *alleviate*… doing something that reduces discomfort. We provide an alternative that will diminish any harsh realities they face.

- We *intoxicate*… offering an artificial distraction to the pain. We lend artificial, even unhealthy means, to distract them from their hurt.

Sadly, these can help kids for a moment but harm them in the end. When we take away pain, we remove their ability to build resistance. Our human capability to deal with pain works like a muscle. Use it or lose it. Our kids' capacity to endure hardship atrophies like a muscle in a cast. When we never exercise that muscle, it atrophies, or shrinks, due to disuse. It's still there, but it becomes weak because it never gets used.

The bottom line? I believe parents must stop acting as their kids' concierge, their personal assistant, and their agent.

--------------------- THE PRINCIPLE ---------------------
When we take away pain, their ability to
endure hardship atrophies.

In 2010, I reported in *Generation iY* that 60 percent of college students were moving back home when they finished with college. Two years later, the *Baltimore Sun* released the 2012 number: 80 percent of college seniors planned to move back home when finished with college. One year later, in 2013, Monster.com upped the number to 85 percent. I recognize we have a tough economy, but it's not that tough. The fact is, the jobs are ready but the graduates are not. Some 53 percent of young adults under 25 are unemployed or underemployed. Many have been crippled by their inability to perform jobs. And about six in ten people between the ages of 18 and 39 who are not students are still receiving financial aid from their parents.[2]

Which of the big four tactics above are you
most prone to use?

Removing Pain Can Lead to Addictions

Have you ever thought that our preoccupation with removing pain just might be a chief reason for addictive behavior? And I'm not simply talking about pills or cigarettes or alcohol. Our culture increasingly demands that we depend on outside sources just to survive the day. It's sending warning signals to me.

> We need meds to go to sleep at night.
>
> We need caffeine to stay alert during the day.
>
> We need music or noise to preoccupy us on our morning commute.
>
> We need entertainment to avoid boredom.
>
> We need alcohol to relax.
>
> We need energy drinks to perform.
>
> We need therapists to prevent depression.
>
> We need Tylenol to remove any aches or discomfort.
>
> We need Facebook to avoid loneliness.
>
> We need more and more government to survive.

And this, to me, is a clear sign of caution. There must be a balance between independence and codependence. No doubt we need each other's gifts and contributions regardless of what we do. That's what commerce and community are all about. But let me ask you a question: Do you need these outside additives just to endure the day?

Forty years ago, a nationwide survey reported that Americans felt they needed 50 possessions in order to live the lifestyle they'd grown accustomed to live. Today, Americans say they need more than 350 items. Somehow, we've drifted. Students today have grown up in a time where they're not learning self-sufficiency. They assume someone else should do things for them. And where did they get that idea? Adults have modeled this for them and done this to them. Somewhere along the way, we morphed into believing that we should mitigate their pain.

Case in point. Prescription drugs are everywhere. Most of us—including me—are glad they're around. Many young people need them to navigate their lives. But today, I fear we have overmedicated our kids, especially our boys. The United States makes up 5 percent of the world's population, but we consume 90 percent of the prescription drugs for ADHD and depression. If they were around today, Charlie Brown would be on Prozac and Dennis the Menace would be on Ritalin.

Boys are taking 30 times more drugs today than in 1987. Are the males really that much worse? That much more needy? Certainly, a kid with ADHD can benefit from proper drugs—medications can even reduce the likelihood of criminal behavior. But many boys continue to take these meds after their bodies have matured. Drugs have prevented young adults from developing their coping skills. In fact, these boys' coping skills likely stopped developing at the age they began taking the meds. We must figure out how to balance prescription drug use with healthy mentoring so males can self-regulate and enter adulthood as healthy young men. I believe there are no shortcuts.[3]

So, can we teach our kids to live well without addictions to meds? In many cases, I believe we can. But it will require a new approach to parenting, teaching, and leading. We will often have to live counterculturally, challenging much of what our world tells us we need. Let me illustrate. Over the years, one of the debates about kids centers on willpower. Is willpower innate? Is it a genetic trait, or can it be taught? The good news is, researchers like Roy Baumeister and Kelly McGonigal at Stanford confirm that willpower can indeed be cultivated and taught—to children as well as adults. We can overcome pain and develop the will to endure. So if this is true, why don't we teach it?

The answer is simple: Our culture doesn't want people with willpower. As Seth Godin writes in *Stop Stealing Dreams*, "Industrialists don't need employees with willpower, and marketers loathe consumers who have it."[4]

A Change of Heart and Mind

We've just identified four specific parental pain-removing tactics, and we've documented the fact that when parents eliminate pain from their children's lives, they reduce their kids' ability to endure even the slightest of hardships. Kids' survival muscles atrophy because of lack of use. I recommend we change our pain-management paradigm. I believe we've confused some realities and weakened our kids' ability to grow into healthy adults. Let me clarify some of the confusion I've heard from parents and teachers.

We mistake hurtful with harmful.

Many times, hurting helps us. In fact, removing the hurt may be harmful. Let that sink in for a moment. When we hurt, we can learn important truths about ourselves and about others, truths that will be beneficial later in our lives. But hurt is different from harm. Harm actually damages us over the long haul. We mistakenly think that if our kids are hurting, they are being harmed, and that's not necessarily so. In fact, it can be quite the opposite.

Think again for a moment about the value of pain. Pain is actually a necessary teacher. For example, consider the constructive connection between pain and your body. If you didn't feel pain, you could severely burn yourself yet remain unaware and not get the medical attention you need. Or you could step on a nail, and by the time you realized it, the infection could have caused permanent damage. The pain of feeling a burn or a puncture is a valuable message from our nerves. It alerts us to take action. Pain (hurt) is an intruder, but it's not our enemy. The pain may feel bad for a moment, but it is actually our best friend in that moment. Pain is a God-given gift. It's helpful—not harmful. However, harm will result if we fail to heed what the pain is telling us to do. Harm happens when we do nothing.

We confuse disturbance with damage.

We hate being disturbed. Our days are so full, we often hope and pray we won't face any unexpected disturbances as we pursue our goals. The fact is, however, that on our way to those goals, we fall into unhealthy ruts. Interruptions force us out of those ruts. Interruptions are not damaging at all. They are the very items that save us from our tunnel vision. We need to be disturbed from time to time. Interruptions are wake-up calls that rouse us from our apathy or complacency.

Pain is not our opponent, and disturbances don't equal damage. Let's try to imagine for a moment that agonizing disturbances may actually save us from truly negative or destructive things. Disturbances can be heralds with important messages—especially for teenagers, who are so insistent on pushing the edge and trying something new or stupid. A critical disturbance may be the guide that gets your kid back on track.

I meet college students all the time who don't drink anymore because they had a run-in with the law and got cited for a DUI. That fateful night led to better decisions in the days that followed. The life-changing disturbance was priceless. Had they been rescued by a parent, they likely would not have changed. Frequently, we do not change until we hurt so much that we *have* to change.

We assume stress is a sickness.

We are raising the most stressed-out generation in recent memory. More kids are on meds for depression and anxiety than any other generation in modern history. If stress is mishandled, it can make us genuinely sick and even cause death. But there is both positive and negative stress. Stress is not inherently evil. Most of us require stress to grow, like a muscle that won't develop without lifting weights. As we said earlier, no pain, no gain. Displacing pain or struggle is different from displacing a disease. If we've raised fragile kids who don't know how to handle difficult times, stress will eventually become an enemy because they won't have any resilience or will. Stress can actually be a good thing if we handle it well.

> If you're basically a low-stress type, but your life is punctuated by short-lived stressors (a.k.a. acute stress), new research suggests that your brain may be the better for it. It seems that acute stress may actually be healthy, since it helps boost the production of new neurons. In particular, neurons may arise in the hippocampus—a part of the brain responsible for memory, and one that is highly sensitive to the effects of stress, both acute and chronic…
>
> Daniela Kaufer said…that stress is not always the culprit we're often led to believe it is. "You always think about

stress as a really bad thing, but it's not. Some amounts of stress are good to push you just to the level of optimal alertness, behavioral and cognitive performance…Stress can be something that makes you better, but it is a question of how much, how long and how you interpret or perceive it."[5]

In short, stress can make us sturdy. Grief can lead to growth.

Common Sense Is Now Uncommon

Let me illustrate how subtle this mistake can be in our adult lives. In October 2013, a surprising news report came out of Port Washington, New York. Worries about injuries at a Long Island middle school led to a ban during recess. Kids can no longer play with footballs, baseballs, soccer balls, or anything else that might hurt someone on school grounds. In fact, playing tag and doing cartwheels without a coach were banned as well.[6] At first, I assumed this was a joke. It's not.

School administrators were concerned about injuries among students and replaced the athletic equipment with Nerf balls. Hmm… makes sense. I'm sure teenagers will love the challenge of playing with a sponge ball on the playground. Yeah, right.

I hope you can see why this is both ridiculous and damaging.

As a dad, I totally understand the desire to keep kids safe. In our effort to reduce injuries, however, we're removing some things that have long been rites of passage for kids in the school community. Needless to say, most students were not thrilled with the news. One said, "You go for recess—and it's our one free time to let loose and recharge." Another student said, "That's all we want to do. We're in school all day sitting behind a desk learning." Another one jumped in: "I think we need the soccer balls, footballs and everything so we can have some fun."

But alas, students will have no such option anymore.

The school superintendent explained that there had been a rash of injuries that warranted this policy. After all, experts say without helmets and pads, kids can get hurt. Educators are simply concerned about the children. (And the lawsuits.)

Why Is This Wrong?

Allow me to make a case for the fact that this policy may prevent kids from getting hurt, but it may increase their chances of being harmed. Educators and parents must beware of the long-term impact of such decisions.

Consider this. When we safeguard kids from getting hurt, they often fail to learn to navigate risk at a young age, when the stakes are relatively low. I'm not suggesting putting helmets or pads on them is wrong, just that protection from hurt hinders them from perceiving the world as it is—and dealing with it. One reason we see teens attempting ridiculous stunts is that many have been so protected as children that they have no clue about the harm risky behavior can bring. Many freshmen in college have never failed, they've never been hurt, they've never shared a room with anyone, and now they don't know how to cope. We did a great job of protecting them from the real world but not so great a job of preparing them for it.

When an 11-year-old boy begins taking medication for ADHD, it helps him cope. He and his whole family get relief. However, he doesn't develop coping skills as other peers do because the meds have intervened. When he stops taking those meds at 18, he will still have the coping skill of an 11-year-old. This makes a job really tough to handle. Or a committed relationship, such as a marriage. Living in his parents' basement until he's 30 sounds really awesome.

I recognize some kids need such medication. I am with thousands of them every year. However, I'm reminding you of the trade-off of such decisions. Each time we intervene in kids' lives, we must develop a way for them to exercise the life skills that may atrophy.

The Price of Our Intervention

When adults intervene like this, we solve short-term problems. I have no doubt that injuries will go down on the playground in that Long Island middle school and all the other schools that have jumped on board with the policy they initiated.

I also have no doubt that preventing hurt today often leads to more harm tomorrow. As kids mature into young adults, they won't be equipped for adulthood. I predict one of two outcomes will emerge:

- The first time they are autonomous, they will try terribly risky behaviors because they've never calculated the negative consequences of stupid conduct.

- They will fear any risk because it's all so new. They never learned to navigate it as children on playgrounds. And they become paralyzed.

Both of these are far more harmful than the hurt of a skinned knee or broken arm as a child. In our effort to prevent hurt, we've accelerated harm. It's now showing up as they become adults. The majority of students today move home after college, feeling ill-equipped for life without help from Mom or Dad. Psychologists in Europe say that some experience phobias because they never faced risk as children. We've already seen that 25-year-olds can experience a quarter-life crisis.

My exhortation is simply this: We must stop leading our kids with short-term vision, and see the long-term impact of our decisions. Hurt is far better than harm. It's common sense.

Learning from Eagles

We should not be surprised that nature furnishes us with vivid pictures of healthy parenting and leadership. Various species of animals instinctively and methodically prepare their young for life. And in so many cases, the process includes the introduction of pain.

Eagles provide one of the most vivid illustrations of this parenting process. For centuries, the eagle has symbolized strong leadership, especially in America, but we often fail to recognize how they lead their young. Four thousand years ago, Moses compared God's leadership of his people to an eagle leading her baby eaglets. He says that God is "like an eagle that stirs up its nest and hovers over its young, that spreads its wings to catch them and carries them aloft" (Deuteronomy 32:11).

Let's break down this process. It progresses from sheltering to show-ing to shoving to shouldering.

The nurturing stage—providing shelter. In this early stage, the mother eagle creates the nest for her babies. With deep care, she plucks and provides her own feathers as lining. She wants to send the message to her young that they are secure and loved deeply.

The disturbance stage—allowing pain. As the eaglets mature a bit, the mother eagle removes the nest's inner lining. She knows it must become uncomfortable, or they'll stay forever. She sends the message that it's time to grow up and not just rest in the nest.

The motivation stage—remaining persistent. At this point, the mother eagle flaps her wings to push the eaglets out of the nest. She incessantly stirs them to make them want to fly. Her message—it's time to get out of the nest and do what you're built to do.

The protection stage—offering safety. As the baby eaglets jump out of the nest, they quickly realize they can't fly yet. Mother flies under the eaglets to catch them as they fall. She will do this until they learn. Her message—you can do this; it is in you to fly.

The success stage—instilling confidence. After several attempts, the eaglets fly on their own. Mother has nurtured them and allowed them to experience pain so they can do what they're intended to do—soar to new heights and have their own babies.

My friend Randy Hain is one of the most intentional fathers I know. He has two sons, and the oldest, Alex, has autism. This special need has made parenting more costly for Randy and his wife. But he knows his job is to prepare his boys for the world that awaits them as adults.

Recently, Randy brought his sons to the annual Growing Leaders donor event. It was a banquet, and everyone sat at tables, ate, mingled, and listened to a presentation. Randy introduced Alex to me before the evening began. The young boy shook my hand and greeted me. I could tell Randy had worked with him on etiquette and social skills. Later, Randy told me something I will never forget. "I know these eve-nings like this can be hard for Alex. Autism makes it difficult for him to sit still, listen, and not call attention to himself. But I want to prepare him for what's ahead, so I look for events like this to be learning times. They're painful, but learning these lessons now is far less painful than the consequences of not learning them until later."

Thanks for saying that, Randy. You are spot-on.

We Do It for Them

Like millions of other people, I frequent Starbucks each week. I love getting a hot skinny vanilla latte on a cold day or a Frappuccino on a warm day. It's something I look forward to as I connect with friends at the end of an afternoon.

Let me tell you something I don't look forward to seeing at those visits to Starbucks. I commonly observe parents sipping coffee as they do their kids' homework. All of it, from math to social studies—daily.

Believe it or not, this happens in Georgia, Michigan, New York, Texas, California…you name it. I know some of these moms and dads. They're part of a new generation of parents who love their children and don't want to see them suffer through the grueling assignments their teachers give them each day. They figure the best way to relieve their kids of the tedious homework is to do it for them.

Tell me, what's wrong with this picture?

After last year's Easter holiday weekend, the *New York Post*, *Good Morning America*, *Fox News*, and other national news sources reported stories of Easter egg hunts that went awry—not due to unruly children, but due to the adults involved.

Joe Allen, founder of *Kids Yule Love*, which organizes his community's egg hunt, said poor behavior made the event a liability because "parents caused a situation in which some children got hurt," the Macon, Georgia, *Telegraph* reported. He said a woman was hurt and several kids were trampled on at previous hunts as aggressive parents tried to get more eggs for themselves or their children.

Organizers said parents were too pushy, leaving some children empty-handed. "When people get hurt, they want some kind of compensation," Allen added.[1] Sadly, it's not the first Easter egg hunt canceled because of pushy parents. An annual event held in Colorado Springs was also canceled because aggressive parents previously snatched too many eggs for their children.

Really? Seriously?

This is a partly humorous, partly sad picture of how adults today are ruining kids. It's no wonder youth cannot seem to grow up when they reach their twenties. They may never have seen a healthy adult role model.

May I say it again? Whether you are a parent, a teacher, a coach, a youth pastor, a school administrator, or an employer, your greatest responsibility to the future is to prepare your kids today to be responsible adults and leaders as they grow up. Susan Peters once said, "Children have a much better chance of growing up if their parents have done so first."

Why Do We Do It?

Now, don't get me wrong. I realize stories of parents doing their kid's homework or snatching up Easter eggs sound a bit far-fetched. But this behavior is illustrative of a new kind of parenting that many have come to embrace—overparenting. The parents take on so much responsibility that they fail to hand over appropriate responsibility to their kids. You and I may never trample children in an Easter egg hunt, but we often do other things that leave our kids ill-equipped for the future. They are often small or subtle things, such as...

- picking up their clothes
- filling out their forms when they're fully capable of doing it
- putting away their toys
- calling their high school teachers or coaches to excuse their behavior
- rescheduling their appointments when they double book their calendar

- resolving their conflicts with their friends

I am a trainer by trade. The organization I lead, Growing Leaders, equips educators and students to think and act like authentic leaders. After three decades of working with students, believe me, I know the temptation to simply say, "Just doing it myself is easier than teaching them to do it."

I also know, however, that our kids are our future. If we leave them ill-equipped for that future because we've given in to that temptation, we've done them a great disservice. Call it what you want, but I think it's a soft form of child abuse. They may love us today because we did so much for them, but will they love us when they're 30 years old and still trying to figure out how to navigate life?

Earlier I referred to the rising number of young adults who still live at home even though they are finished with school. In 2012, 36 percent of our nation's young adults ages 18 to 31 were living in their parents' home, according to a Pew Research Center analysis of US Census Bureau data. This is the highest share in at least four decades and represents a slow but steady increase since before the Great Recession in 2008.

According to one poll, one in four parents say it's okay for their adult children to live with them as long as they want.[2] Once again, I have to wonder, is this sentiment about our needs or theirs? Do our kids really want to stay with us this long, or are we making it too easy for them to fail doing life on their own? I love our two adult children. I was fine when our daughter, Bethany, lived with us for several months once she finished college. But she returned with a plan for moving forward and followed through. There's a difference between moving home with a plan and moving in without one. Those without a plan need a parent to help them create one.

As I host focus groups to find why so many of us are doing things for our kids, I've concluded it's the proverbial pendulum swing. A large population of Baby Boomer (born between 1946 and 1964) and Generation X (born between 1965 and 1983) parents grew up in unhealthy homes. I'm not suggesting that all of our moms and dads were dysfunctional, but that many were consumed with their jobs or their own needs. Many parents were emotionally or physically absent from their children.

It's not surprising that parents today are committed to doing things differently. We don't want to be emotionally absent or disengaged from our kids, so we push the pendulum to the other extreme. We are often overengaged, doing so much for our children that we prevent them from learning important life lessons. It's as if we're committed to ensuring our adult children don't need to see a counselor when they're 30 years old (because Mom and Dad weren't there for them), so we overdo our responsibilities. We fail them when the time comes for them to leave us. They're unprepared.

The Price Tag

Parents who do too much for their children invite these results:

We don't experience the satisfaction of training them for adulthood.

Few things are more fulfilling than actually equipping a child to do an adult task, whether mowing the lawn, changing the oil in a car, paying bills, or making a big purchase. If you think doing something for your kids is nice, wait until you actually train them to do it for themselves. It's exhilarating.

Our children become lazy and unmotivated.

Doing too much for our children actually fosters an entitlement mentality. Kids begin believing they deserve to have someone in their life who always takes care of them. Soon, they assume they will be rescued, so they never cultivate incentive to work or serve others. They're unable to motivate themselves to initiate a step of progress.

The world around them doesn't receive what they have to offer.

Consider this consequence of doing too much for your kids. When we don't prepare them to do life on their own, problems go unsolved that they could have solved if they had applied their talents. If they fail to use their gifts, hundreds if not thousands of others suffer the consequences.

Our kids become disabled and don't reach their potential.

This may be the heaviest consequence of all. When we do things for our kids, we can actually disable them. Think about it. They won't learn to swim in a pool by reading a book about it or watching us do it. They must get into the water themselves and do it. If they don't, they're not swimmers. So it is with life.

Training is ultimate parenting. Dwight Moody once said, "It's better to train a hundred people than to do the work of a hundred people. But…it's harder."

THE PRINCIPLE

When we do things for them, they can become lazy, unmotivated to grow, and disabled.

When Helping Our Kids Starts Hurting Them

Let me ask you a question. How far would you go to help your kid do well in school? If you're a teacher, how much do you do to help your kids score well on tests?

More and more, adults worldwide are demonstrating they're willing to go to almost any length to help kids, all in the name of love. "I love those kids," we say.

Recently, a 52-year-old mother was caught helping her teenage daughter cheat on an exam. She didn't just help her—she took the test for her daughter. Yep. She allegedly showed up and took a crucial exam, wearing low-cut jeans, Converse shoes, and lots of makeup to blend in at the exam center in Paris, France.

According to the *Telegraph*, the test center was not at her 19-year-old daughter's school, and there were nontraditional students (adults) also taking the test, so no one noticed her at first. Eventually, the mom was spotted by a teacher who knew the teen, and police were called to escort her out of the building. She now faces a fine of $11,800 and three years in prison. Her daughter may not be able to retake any official state test for five years.[3] Incredible.

May I suggest the bigger crime?

We can be tempted to step in and help our kids on any level, but doing this is a trade-off at best. We no doubt relieve them of stress in the moment, but we may enable them to fail in the end. They never develop resilience. One day, we will not be next to them to help them. What skill will they have then—cheating skills or problem-solving skills? This kind of "help" not only communicates to kids that cheating to get what you want is okay, it disables them from building life skills.

Endurance and perseverance are nonexistent when kids don't learn to struggle through adversity to solve problems. As I've said, when we consistently do things for our kids, they can become lazy, unmotivated to grow, and even disabled from learning to live independently. The bigger crime is that we cheat our children out of long-term success and growth in their lives. Life skills atrophy because those emotional muscles never get developed. Whether we know it or not, helping them in this way screams a terrible message: "I must help you because you are incapable."

This can continue even when our kids go off to college. According to a recent study, parents who provide total support of their college son or daughter may do damage as well as good.

> The study, published in...*American Sociological Review*, suggests students with some of their own "skin in the game" may work harder, and that students with parents picking up more of the tab are free to take on a more active social and extracurricular life. That may be fun and even worthwhile, but comes at a cost to GPA...
>
> The findings don't suggest parents should stop supporting students financially...But they should lay out standards and expectations. And even if parents can afford the whole bill, it may be worthwhile to make students put up some of their own funds or work part-time, so they feel invested.[4]

This often feels weird to us. Many of us feel we've failed if we do not pay for our kids' college education. We assume we must do it for them even when they're in their twenties. This kind of paternal perspective is solidified when our children are K-12 students and simply need help with homework or school projects. We feel it's our duty. When we jump in and do it for them, we signal once again, "You won't make it without me."

Is this what we want to communicate? There must be a better way to help them. So let's begin to resist this urge to do it for them by taking this EASY path.

E—Encourage them first.

The best help a parent can offer first is to sit down and offer encouragement. Kids need to hear someone they respect tell them, "I think it's in you to do this. You have what it takes." Encouragement is the oxygen of the soul.

A—Ask questions next.

Look at problems with your children. Ask them questions that will help them do the critical thinking they need to do to solve it. Asking questions is almost always more helpful than spoon-feeding kids possible answers. It teaches them how to think.

S—Simulate a problem.

Come up with a similar problem and walk them through it. This helps them develop a skill they can apply to problems they've been given by their instructor. In other words, instead of merely talking about it, help them practice the skill they must learn.

Y—Yoke them with a peer.

Like oxen in a yoke together, connect them to other students who do understand the work. Yokes enable two oxen, a weaker and stronger one, to work together. Build a bridge to a solution through a peer rather than doing the work for them.

Is your child experiencing a current situation
where you could practice these steps?

It Can Be Done!

My friend Andy told me his ten-year-old son, Wyatt, was struggling to keep up in his math class. At the end of the semester, when Andy asked Wyatt how he was doing, Wyatt broke down in tears. He had failed an exam, so he was the only kid who didn't get to go to a class pizza party. Andy made a decision to not march down to the school and try to make the problem go away. Instead, he decided to encourage Wyatt, and he asked where he needed help. By the end of their conversation, Wyatt told his father he never wanted to miss another pizza party again. Determined to succeed, he went online and signed up for a mentor at Mathnasium. Thanks to a great dad, Wyatt is improving at both math and life skills. Not bad for a ten-year-old kid.

Lenore Skenazy's *Free Range Kids* tracks the stories of how we're failing to prepare our children for leadership.[5] Many parents in the United States seem to be convinced that children are incapable of making any of their own decisions or even functioning by themselves at the playground. While a high school principal recently threatened to suspend a group of seniors for the dangerous act of riding their bikes to school, and a group of parents protested that their misbehaving 17- to 18-year-olds were sent home alone on a train, schools in Europe have 4-year-olds walking to school by themselves and teenagers also traveling alone across Europe and handling transactions with different currency and in different languages. It can be done. Our kids can do it—if we'll only let them.

The truth is, kids can do more than we could ever imagine. We often don't see it because we just haven't led them well. The key is to harness their imagination and willpower. I recently met Dr. Elena Bodrova, coauthor of *Tools of the Mind*. She and her colleague, Deborah Leong, completed research on preschool-age children and proved that they are capable of self-control and discipline. Instead of pushing kids to do something, they are cultivating self-guided minds.

Let me illustrate. In one famous study, kids were told to stand still as long as they could. They lasted two minutes. Then a second group was told to pretend they were soldiers on guard who had to stand still at their posts. They lasted eleven minutes. It's about changing conduct from the inside out. *Tools of the Mind* challenges kids to learn abstract thinking, using their imaginations. They end up writing better, socializing better, and even sitting still longer. The point is, they are able to do what adults felt they could not do. But we must equip them to do it![6]

What Really Cultivates Happy Kids?

As I've mentioned before, parents have intuitively felt that lots of affirmation and care builds self-esteem in children. This is why millions of moms and dads compliment their kids for every little thing they do. But since the self-esteem movement has taken root in America over the past 40 years, we have learned an important truth. Affirmation alone does not breed self-esteem. It breeds narcissism.

Dr. Jean Twenge has overseen a longitudinal study of college students that dates back to the 1970s. She tells us narcissism continues to climb as parents dote over their children, validating their every move and telling them they're special. In the 1950s, when teens were asked, "Are you a very important person?" less than 10 percent said they were. Fifty years later, more than 80 percent said they were. Unfortunately, they continue to show signs of depression, angst, and poor self-esteem when it comes to risk taking and responsibility. Something is wrong.

We've found that children's strength and self-esteem rise when parents are responsive as well as demanding. Parents are responsive by offering encouragement, belief, understanding, and support. They are demanding by setting standards and holding kids accountable to them.

Believe it or not, genuine self-esteem is built from achievement, not just affirmation. Kids need to feel they can accomplish something with their own skill set. When adults do things for their kids, over time they send the message, "You are unable. I must do this." Eventually, even good kids will begin to feel poorly about themselves. They may hide behind a facade of pride and confidence, but inside they may be experiencing what psychologists call "high arrogance, low self-esteem." By the time they are ten years old, kids must gain a sense of pride through accomplishment ("I performed with excellence in my gift area") and through effort ("Even if I didn't achieve, I know I gave my best effort"). Having kids' beds made perfectly each morning isn't nearly as important as having kids who know how to make their own beds.

Ron and Melanie are parents of a teenage daughter named Melissa. They've admitted to me that they've been guilty of doing far too much for their daughter. As Melissa entered her teenage years, she grew overweight and selfish, and she felt entitled to own nice clothes, smartphones, tablets…you name it. Needless to say, she was less fun to be around for both family and friends.

This led to Melissa making poor decisions just to get a guy to like her. To make a long story short, Melissa got pregnant. The situation was a crucible for her and the entire family. Once she had her baby, Mom and Dad continued to do things for her, but they eventually grew exhausted. They couldn't do it all. Things had to change. Melissa finally had to own her choices and grow up. Ron and Melanie continued to offer support and belief, but they stopped doing so many things for her—and Melissa became a changed young woman. As she took more responsibility, she soon became happier. While it felt counterintuitive, the less Ron and Melanie did for their daughter, the better things got. Melissa took initiative with tasks, helped out around the house, lost 60 pounds, and feels great.

Hmm…I don't believe this is a coincidence. Kids need you to be responsive *and* demanding. And in the end, they are happier with themselves.

Then and Now

Imagine for a moment this scenario.

Parents are trying hard to take control of their homes. The world in which they're raising their children is entirely different from the world they knew as kids. Technology is playing a larger role than ever before. Kids are growing up in front of screens—for hours each day. The programs and music these kids consume are so different than they were in past generations. Kids seem to be out of control, with no respect for tradition and no thought of long-term consequences to their decisions. What is a parent to do?

Sound familiar to you?

This is actually a description of society when the Baby Boomers were growing up. The boom happened after World War II, when our nation went through adolescence. The music was strange, just as adults feel it is today. The kids thought outside the box, just as adults believe kids do today. And the screens—which now appear on smartphones, tablets, and laptops—were once television screens.

Adults had never raised kids in this new world, so they were at a loss as to how to parent, teach, or lead them. In fact, in many ways, the adults backed off from leading them at all. Dr. Benjamin Spock suggested that children were "little people" who should not be spanked, but allowed to express themselves. And boy, did those Baby Boomers express themselves. It was a strange time because there was no compass for the journey through this uncharted territory.

Today, history has repeated itself.

Back in the 1960s, some parents were wary of the TV set, suspecting that it was evil and that it would influence their children to do bad things. (Some traditionalists even referred to TV as "hellevision.") On the other extreme, some parents just didn't know how to handle this new piece of technology that allowed culture to seep in and impact their kids' thinking and values. So they threw up their hands and gave up trying to corral them.

Culture won. The device became the one-eyed babysitter, and prevailed.

The answer, of course, was somewhere in the middle. Parents eventually recognized that TV was neutral, neither good nor evil. The programming was the real issue. Wise moms and dads began to offer guidance as to how to make good decisions on viewing. Once their kids had a moral compass to make these choices, the screen in their life didn't control them—they knew how to control it.

This is the lesson we must learn today.

We parents and teachers are raising a generation of kids inundated with a new wave of technology, much like the generation of 50 years ago. Once again, there are no rules of engagement for this new technology.

Our mantra was TGIF—Thank God It's Friday. Dr. Leonard Sweet reminds us that today's mantra is also TGIF—Twitter, Google, Instagram, and Facebook.

A New GPS

In the same way we need directions and a GPS when traveling in new territory, we need directions to guide young people in today's uncharted terrain. In fact, we must provide a moral compass to help kids determine their true north. Then we must offer guidelines for them, much like an interpersonal GPS.

In retrospect, I wonder if the parents of the Baby Boomers would say they were at a loss and perhaps didn't lead the Boomer generation into adulthood well. The mantra of that young generation during the 1960s was Question Authority. We began using the term *generation gap*. There was a divide between adults and youth. Singer Bob Dylan warned, "Never trust anyone over 30." It seems parents were failing to do enough for their kids.

Today our challenge is the opposite—we do too much. In this new world, we're so fearful of life's uncertainties, we figure we'd better just do it all for our children. Truthfully, the answer again is likely in the middle. We must do something but not too much.

We have an advantage today. Students seem to want to stay connected to parents and caring adults. We have an opportunity to provide them with a GPS for this new world. Knowing that technology is not going away, we owe it to our young people to help them navigate this new world so they can capitalize on all it offers but not lose the life skills that may atrophy as they do.

May I suggest some action steps?

Get acquainted with the latest technology.

Stay current and understand what devices are available, especially ones your kids enjoy using. Recognize the benefits and the liabilities of using them. What do they help us do more efficiently? What life skills may diminish as we use them? For example, we all love high-speed Internet, but are we becoming less patient people because of it?

Determine what timeless virtues and life skills are important.

Sit down and talk with your kids (or students) and list the life skills you think are valuable in a career and a family. This will help you clarify what your compass is and what you don't want to surrender in the name of technology.

Agree on boundaries that will enable kids to become well-rounded adults.

This means teaching kids to take advantage of technology but to control it rather than be controlled by it. For example, a male may want to break up with his girlfriend through a text message. But is that appropriate, or should he develop conflict-resolution skills and do it face-to-face? Here are some starter questions for you to talk about.

- Does communicating for hours on Facebook diminish my people skills?
- If all my conversations are texts, do I still learn to read body language?
- If a screen dominates my day, can I still develop emotional intelligence?
- With all the external stimulation, how do I cultivate internal motivation?
- With the conveniences of ATMs, microwaves, and instant messaging, am I still able to delay gratification?

Recognize that all growth comes from conditioning.

Athletes develop muscles through strength and conditioning. They have strength coaches to help them do it. The opposite of conditioning is atrophy. Muscles shrink when they don't get used. The purpose of guiding kids and curbing technology is merely to prevent important life skills and virtues from atrophying.

> Can you walk through this process and
> help your child develop a personal GPS?

Resourcefulness and Resilience

In 2005, Bradford Smart wrote a book called *Topgrading*. It is full of insights on how to hire, develop, and keep A-level players on your team. In the midst of the message, Smart suggests that in the world of tomorrow, resourcefulness is king. Let me summarize and explain this message and then apply it to our kids.

Smart says that resourcefulness is the new metacompetency as employees enter the workforce. Think about it. Information is ubiquitous, so we no longer need people who know a lot. Information is readily available. You can search and find answers to almost any problem if you know where to look. That's why the virtue of resourcefulness is now the most important skill to build and find. I'm talking about people who know how to find answers, ones who can identify and solve problems because they can find solutions far beyond our current practice. Resourceful people can...

- comprehend the key problems that slow down progress
- search for and find ideas they can connect to those problems
- develop a series of solutions to the problems
- modify and implement the best solutions[7]

As you parent and teach your children, this is a profound truth to understand. To give kids an advantage as they mature into adulthood, we must equip them to be resourceful, to not shrink from digging into issues and drawing conclusions about them, to know how to search for and find answers for themselves. At Growing Leaders, we hire young staff members who possess this skill. They are resourceful as they connect ideas, create new systems, and tweak ideas others have used somewhere else. They are priceless. Somewhere along the way, someone helped them to become resourceful.

In addition, there is one more valuable commodity we must intentionally build into our children's lives—resilience. The speed and convenience that mark our culture have diminished the virtue of resilience. Nationwide, teachers report that young people today give up too easily. They don't like problems that take too long or require too much effort to solve. I believe resilience is a second priceless competency after resourcefulness. Both are lacking in Generation iY.

We surveyed more than 8000 students this past year and discovered resilience is a rare commodity among teens. And it is declining. Resilience is the ability to bounce back after adversity. Technology has made life quick and easy, so parents, coaches, and teachers must find ways to develop resilience in our kids.

These are students' top remarks to their K-12 teachers:

> "This is too hard."
>
> "I need help."
>
> "I can't do this."

Could it be we failed to prepare them to do the hard thing themselves?

It's as Easy as Riding a Bike

Allow me to close with an analogy. Just as a child cannot learn to swim by watching someone do it, neither can a child learn to ride a bicycle through observation alone. These are things they must learn by doing them themselves.

Do you recall teaching your kids to ride a bike? I was reflecting recently with a group of school principals about what this experience teaches us about leading kids and developing student leaders.

Consider the phases in learning to ride a bike. At first, you were far too young to ride the bike yourself. You were just a toddler, so Mom or Dad positioned you behind them or strapped you onto their lap, *on their bike*, and took you for ride. It was exhilarating to feel the wind in your face and not have a care in the world. You concluded then that bikes were cool, and you could hardly wait to ride one yourself.

Next, you finally got your own bike. It was only a tricycle, but still—it was yours. You took that little set of wheels out on the driveway and got used to going solo. Of course, it was bike riding on a miniature scale, but you had the experience of climbing on, accelerating, steering, and braking all by yourself. You were satisfied for a while, but as you grew, eventually you knew you had to get one of those big bikes.

Then you finally got one. It was an actual bicycle with two wheels instead of three. Maybe it had cool handlebars or streamers or spokes, and it was uniquely yours. There was just one caveat. You were scared to death to get on it. So one of your parents explained that you learn to ride a two-wheeler by using training wheels.

But eventually, that too grew old, and one day you asked Dad to take off the training wheels. You were feeling a little embarrassed by them—after all, you may have been five or six years old. Dad joined you in the garage, pulled a crescent wrench from his toolbox, and removed the training wheels.

Suddenly you got butterflies in your stomach. But Dad assured you that he'd support you as you pedaled that bike with no extra wheels. It took you a few times and a couple of skinned knees, but you eventually got it mastered. But do you realize what your parent had to do to get you to that point?

It was a beautiful combination of support and letting go.

This narrative is a picture of what we must experience as we lead kids. At first, we do it all. They're riding on our bikes and get a taste of what good leadership feels like. Then they get their own trike, taking on a small responsibility of their own. No big risk, but it's important for them to do it on their own. Next, they own a big bike. They take on a significant role, but we give them training wheels by offering support and accountability, ensuring they won't kill themselves or anyone else as they lead. They're finally ready to become adults—leaders—when we offer a tender balance of support and letting go. Too much of either and we have an accident. In the end, we must take our hands off and let them ride.

One last thought. Once they begin riding their own leadership bike, they may go down a road you never intended them to ride on. It wasn't in your plan. Are you okay with letting them create their own path? Are you prepared to perhaps allow them to fall down along the way and learn what roads are best without forcing your map on them?

May you take this journey with your kids and become a great bike-riding instructor.

We Prepare the Path for the Child Instead of the Child for the Path

I recently spoke at the commencement for a university in South Carolina. The president, who is a great friend of mine, said he knew of some mothers and fathers who refused to believe their children were not graduating with honors. After all, their children were special and deserved to be recognized as special. So what did those parents do? You might not believe this. They created their own set of honor cords and tassels for their children to wear at their graduation.

Wow. I wonder if the grads were embarrassed.

My colleague Elise Fowler just told me about a parent–teacher meeting that took place recently at her local middle school. She was appalled at their announcements.

- There is no F in the grading system anymore. U (unsatisfactory) is the new F. Students can turn in homework and projects anytime during the semester and still receive full credit.

- If students make a U on a test, they can retake that test as many times as they need to until they pass. The only requirement is that they have to go to at least one tutoring session.

How are these changes preparing students for the real world, where they will have to deal with failure, deadlines, and missed opportunities? This is one reason our work at Growing Leaders is so critical.

Unfortunately, kids are not getting leadership at school unless passionate parents, teachers, and administrators take the lead in delivering it. I hate to sound old-fashioned, but we are truly living in a different era in which many school systems won't let students fail. They can keep trying until they pass, and we push them through the system. I fear the standard of academic excellence and emotional intelligence for students is slowly being replaced with a satisfaction with mediocrity. Just get them through.

In the fall of 2013, a report went viral about a soccer league in Ontario, Canada. Adults decided that in order to ensure that every kid wins, they would simply do away with the ball. Kids would have to use their imagination, and coaches would simply say the game was tied at the end. The following day, the story was exposed as a hoax, but the fact that the report went viral demonstrates how far we've come as a society. People actually believed the story. Whether they liked it or not—it got news attention. Fifty years ago, no one would have bought it.[1]

The Bottom Line

I will confess, in my children's early days, I prepared the path for the child. I made it easy for my son to hit the baseball, I hid Easter eggs in easy-to-spot places, I gave them head starts in races. In early childhood, this gives them confidence. Once they finish elementary school, however, this strategy eventually backfires. Kids will cultivate unrealistic expectations of how easy life is and how superior they are to other kids. When we continue to pave the way for them in childhood, they fail to develop perspective and won't be ready for the rigor of real life.

In short, preparing the path for the child is not helpful. When we do this, we actually sell our kids short. We fail to call out the very best in them, assuming we must smooth the road and make things easy for them. When we do so, life feels good to them on the outside (it's easier), but it doesn't feel good on the inside (they don't respect themselves). As they age, they see a widening gap between how they live and the real world. We actually make it harder for them to reach their potential.

In contrast, I believe our young people are capable of so much more than they are currently showing us. It is in them to do great things—we just haven't expected it. Our kids are capable to be and do more than we imagine—certainly more than getting lost on Facebook and Twitter. The truth is, we often dumb down life.

When we make this mistake, their childhood works fine, but their adulthood looks bleak. I liken it to running a marathon without preparing but expecting to finish well. Too often, we prepare our kids for a sprint in life, not a distance race. Life is a marathon, not a sprint. The more we can do to equip kids for it, the better. And this means preparing *them*, not the path they take.

THE PRINCIPLE

Preparing the path for your children
fails to prepare them for life.

A Skewed Parental Scorecard

There's a reason we tend to do this. Many of us parents now have a new scorecard we use to evaluate our success.

We win if we provide ease and comfort for our kids.

Maybe we do this because it's the only way we know. Perhaps our own parents weren't good role models; they weren't strong in preparing us for adulthood. If we haven't seen examples of good training, we intuitively nurture and coddle our kids. Our scorecard is based simply on providing well for our kids.

We win if our kids love and adore us.

It could be we yearn so much to be loved by our children, we dare not upset them. We're insecure and need their approval. We don't want them to turn on us. This means we make life easy for them. It's all about earning their love. Remember, if you need your kids to like you, you won't parent well. Our need will skew our perspective.

We win if we survive the day or the week.

Many of us relate to this. At the end of a day, we're just plain tired.

We slip into survival mode, and training or preparing our kids to do something is the last thing on our mind. And even if we did think of it, we wouldn't know how. We can't see past today. We're just happy to make it through the week.

We win if our kids feel enough love.

I've mentioned this before. I've found many parents who fear their kids will be seeing a therapist as adults because they never received enough love or nurture. This blinds us from their future needs. We constantly react to their needs today, so we do more protecting and less preparing.

Question: What items are on your parenting scorecard?
How do you measure success?

The World Is Changing

It's been said so often, it sounds cliché. The world is changing rapidly, and it's actually affecting the way we raise and teach our children. We are no longer living in the industrial age. The information age has been upon us for decades and is giving way to version 2.0. I've said it before—we are raising the first generation of kids that doesn't need adults to get information. Data is everywhere. We must move away from seeing ourselves as the dispensers of content. They don't need us for *information* but for *interpretation*. We must help them make sense of what they know. To mentor kids is to provide them with a healthy worldview, not just to require them to memorize facts the way we had to do in school. They don't need us to access information, but to process it. I love the way culture guru Seth Godin puts it:

> I believe memorizing the year that the Battle of Hastings was fought is trivia. On the other hand, understanding the sweep of history, being able to visualize the repeating cycles of conquest and failure, and having an innate

understanding of the underlying economics of the world are essential insights for educated people to understand.[2]

I believe every teacher, parent, coach, youth pastor, and employer ought to ask this question as they work with young people: Is this class/program/task/rule created to help our students do the same old thing and remain children, or are we opening a new door for them to do something new and grow from it?

We don't need to create more compliant children who've memorized data. We need to build a generation of creative and motivated leaders who can pave the way into our future. To do this, we build fundamental skill sets inside of them that are marked by both dreaming and discipline. This means we must stretch them.

The Biggest Predictor of Success in Life

You may remember the famous marshmallow test performed nearly half a century ago at Stanford University. (You can find an amusing reenactment of it on YouTube.)

In the experiment, psychologist Walter Mischel seated young children (one at a time) in a room, placed a marshmallow on a table in front of them, and said he would return in 15 minutes. He told the children they could eat the marshmallow anytime they wished, but if they waited until he returned, they'd get two marshmallows. The results are entertaining to watch. Many of the kids just couldn't wait. Others looked it over, sniffed it, touched it to their lips…but waited to eat it.

The fascinating outcomes showed up years later in the early 1980s. Researchers tracked down those same kids as young adults and discovered the ones who were able to wait for two marshmallows at age four had much higher SAT scores and better academic records as teens. These results are sparking new thinking on what helps kids succeed in school and in life—and it isn't always a high IQ. Instead, it's noncognitive skills, such as the ability to delay gratification. In fact, researchers now say that "executive function" skills, such as self-control, perseverance, patience, and long-term flexible thinking, enable kids to flourish.

May I comment to you parents, teachers, coaches, and youth workers? I understand our desire to improve standardized test scores, but we have a large population of kids who've figured out how to take a test but not how to make it on a job or in a marriage. Our children are not stupid. They have enough savvy to calculate what they must do to get by in classrooms they deem irrelevant.

The truth is, our kids graduate and still lack the soft skills they need to get hired. According to two nationwide surveys, HR executives report a skills gap in the graduates they've interviewed. Most of their young job candidates were turned down. Half of their job openings remained unfilled. In short, the jobs are ready, but the kids aren't.

To address this issue, the television show *Sesame Street* has gotten into the act. This past year, they brought on a writer to introduce executive function skills to the script. Appropriately, they chose Cookie Monster to be their poster child for learning to delay gratification. Think about it—in the past, when Cookie Monster wanted a cookie, he got a cookie. Now we can watch him learn to wait and perhaps get two of them. He's developing executive function skills as a good Muppet monster should. I love it.

So, what can we do to cultivate these executive functions in our children?

Expand the scorecard for your kids.

In addition to good grades, why not reward attitude and soft skills like delaying gratification, grit, or effort? Let your young people know these are what count as an adult, employee, or leader. Remember, what gets rewarded gets repeated.

Gamify the process.

Find ways to turn the development of those soft skills into a game or competition. This can be done with computers, points, prizes, and laughter. As Mary Poppins said, "In every job that must be done, there is an element of fun."

Give them opportunities to practice soft skills.

At our house, our children helped us host parties for our adult friends. They learned to greet adults at the door, take their coats, introduce them to other adults, get them iced tea, and more. It was a preparation for life.

Simulate the grind of adulthood.

Create ways to simulate job interviews, conflict resolution, or discipline. One week, I asked my kids to think of two things they hated to do—and challenged them to do those things daily for a week. Chores or service projects can become good habits.

Incentivize waiting.

Patience is almost a lost virtue, even in adults. It's like we're all pacing in front of our microwave ovens. So when your young people want something, raise the stakes and offer a huge reward if they'll wait two months for it. Remember the marshmallows.

Tell lots of stories.

I know you think kids are tired of you talking about the good old days. But I've found most kids love hearing stories of how we adults struggled to learn these same life skills when we were young. It's all part of growing up.

I just got a call from a former intern. He served on our team one summer while in college. He told me he simply wanted to apologize for being so immature during that summer and to say how much he appreciated the initiation into the real world he'd gotten from our team. Although he was very intelligent, he declared the summer experience was equal to his entire college career, and it had helped him thrive in his new job. He's now a grateful 23-year-old.

He needed more than a classroom on his pathway to success.

The Sudbury Valley School was founded more than 40 years ago, during the Baby Boomer era of hippies and free love. Here is part of the foundation for their school.

The way we saw it, responsibility means that each person has to carry the ball for himself. You, and you alone, must make your decisions, and you must live with them. No one should be thinking for you, and no one should be protecting you from the consequences of your actions. This, we felt, is essential if you want to be independent, self-directed, and the master of your own destiny.[3]

The Struggle Between Our Head and Our Heart

As I researched for this chapter, I found myself thinking this makes sense, but it is so hard to watch our kids struggle with fear and angst. We know better than to make things easy, but somehow we assume their self-esteem will be stronger if we smooth the path for them. As I continued digging, however, even this excuse was shot down. Consider this article excerpt, which draws from the work of Edward Hallowell, author of *The Childhood Roots of Adult Happiness.*

> If you really want to bolster your child's self-esteem, focus less on compliments and more on providing her with ample opportunities to learn new skills. Mastery, not praise, is the real self-esteem builder, Dr. Hallowell says. Fortunately, when it comes to the under-4 crowd, nearly everything they do is a chance to attain mastery—because it's all new to them: learning to crawl, walk, feed and dress themselves, use the potty, and ride a tricycle. Our challenge is to stand back and let our children do for themselves what they're capable of. "The great mistake good parents make is doing too much for their children," Dr. Hallowell says.
>
> While it can be difficult to watch our kids struggle, they'll never know the thrill of mastery unless we allow them to risk failure. Few skills are perfected on a first try. It's through practice that children achieve mastery. And through repeated experiences of mastery, they develop the can-do attitude that lets them approach future challenges with the zest and optimism that are central to a happy life.[4]

I have a hunch. If I were to ask parents why they prepare the path for their kids, they would probably reply, "I want them to be happy today." They know it may not be in their kids' best interest over the long haul, but we're parenting in the now.

> It sounds counterintuitive, but the best thing you can do for your child's long-term happiness may be to stop trying to keep her happy in the short-term. "If we put our kids in a bubble and grant them their every wish and desire, that is what they grow to expect, but the real world doesn't work that way," says author Bonnie Harris, founder of Core Parenting…
>
> To keep from overcoddling, recognize that you are not responsible for your child's happiness, Harris urges. Parents who feel responsible for their kids' emotions have great difficulty allowing them to experience anger, sadness, or frustration. We swoop in immediately to give them whatever we think will bring a smile or to solve whatever is causing them distress. Unfortunately, Harris warns, children who never learn to deal with negative emotions are in danger of being crushed by them as adolescents and adults.[5]

I will be honest with you. As I meet with hundreds of parents each year and speak to thousands of them, I continue to see a trend. I mentioned it earlier in this book. It is our predisposition to want to be in control. Some of us are extreme cases—we are control freaks. This plays out in our parenting through our attempts to manage and manipulate our children's friendships, their activities, the clothes they wear, their hobbies, who their teachers are in school, their college, even their dreams.

I know—doing this has crossed my mind a time or two. After all, these kids are our offspring. Why wouldn't we want to control their lives? We know better than they do. This backfires, of course, because control is a myth. Even though you may have given birth to these children, they were born with their own mind, opinions, feelings, and goals. Seeking to control their lives is like seeking to control the wind.

We cannot. All we can do is harness the way we respond to the wind, like a good sailor on a ship. And this begins with surrendering our control over their happiness.

> Once you accept that you can't make your child feel happiness (or any other emotion for that matter), you'll be less inclined to try to "fix" her feelings—and more likely to step back and allow her to develop the coping skills and resilience she'll need to bounce back from life's inevitable setbacks.[6]

The fact of the matter is, for many of life's situations, control is a myth. There are very few things that we control. The sooner we recognize this, the more effectively we will lead our children. As a parent, I must always remember that everything happening to my child falls into one of three categories:

- Situations that are in my control—I must take responsibility for these.
- Situations that are out of my control—I must trust others and stop worrying.
- Situations that are within my influence—I must respond by acting wisely.

Along the parenting journey, I will encounter some situations that are within my control, such as my attitude toward them, the food they eat at home, the love I display, the home and resources I provide, and the example I set. I must not blame others for the way these work out, and I must not expect others to assume responsibility for them. Instead I must take responsibility for these. I must recognize my role and be proactive about fulfilling it.

When I encounter situations that are out of my control, my worst reaction is to force my way in and manipulate them. A vast number of these circumstances tempt me to step in and try to control—the way other kids treat my child, the kind of teacher my kid gets, my child's attitude toward me, how happy, talented, smart, or beautiful my kid is…you get the picture. These aren't for me to control.

When I encounter situations that are within my influence, I must respond wisely, balancing the temptation to control the situation with the temptation to sit back and do nothing. These situations include helping my child develop a healthy worldview, enabling my child to be prepared for challenges, preparing my kid to relate well to others and to know what is right, equipping my child to work hard, and so on. I hope you can see the slight difference between this category and the items in your control. You cannot control your child's attitude, but you can influence it. You cannot do the job interview for her, but you can prepare her for it. Influence is not control.

Question: Do you try to control your child's
life and happiness?

Bringing Out the Best in Your Kids

So how do we appropriately influence our kids? How do we transform our kids and our homes so they are consistently peaceful? How do we give up our ambition for control and allow our children to endure some hardship so they can grow up? How do we shift to less of us and more of them?

Let me remind you that most positive changes don't happen overnight. It's best to start slow and small. Baby steps, as they say. For instance, if your kids display a sense of entitlement with low attention spans and little patience, the answer is not to suddenly become harsh and demand that they grow up. We may well need to stop coddling or spoiling our kids and introduce them to the real world, but to go quickly from tender to tough won't work. The shock would push them away. It would be like exiting a dark cinema after a movie and walking outside into the daylight. We quickly shut our eyes and want to go back inside. The light is too harsh. We must intentionally ease them onto a path to maturity. Slow and small. Over the years, I have noticed the effect of adults who lead too softly or too harshly. The outcomes look something like this.

If we got whatever we wanted and felt loved, we became spoiled.

When I was a kid, parents took pride in providing their children with whatever they needed. Today, many parents seem to take pride in giving their kids whatever they want. We seem to think that's the job of good parents. This is a sad and unhealthy shift. Part of the reason some kids possess a sense of entitlement is that adults have communicated that the kids deserve whatever they want—the newest iPad, smartphone, app for that phone, name-brand clothes…you name it. When we express our love for our kids this way, we set them on a path to act spoiled. They often become entitled adults as a result. They become brats that others don't enjoy being around.

If we got whatever we wanted but did not feel loved, we became superficial.

I see another scenario in homes. In these families, kids enjoy all the new stuff available in stores but still question whether they are really loved. These are often two-income homes. Mom and dad are busy all the time, so they come home tired and compensate for their lack of time and energy by simply buying the latest clothes and technology. This is a classic Baby Boomer approach—to simply throw money at the problem. It's tempting, especially if you have the money. The children enjoy the latest gadgets, but sometimes they look past all the possessions and wonder if Mom and Dad love them or even want to spend time with them. They see time as more valuable than money, knowing you can always get more money but you can never get more time. Life has become about owning things, and they try to win that game but often become superficial with their relationships. They don't know how to go deep, so they stick to the surface whether they're online or talking face-to-face.

If we did not get whatever we wanted but still felt loved, we became secure.

In the healthiest scenario for kids, parents find authentic ways to communicate their love for their children, but they don't give their kids every single thing their kids want. Over time, this wonderful scenario communicates to the children that Mom and Dad love them so much, they have set parameters to guide the children's development. As I mentioned earlier, security is the result of consistent leadership and boundaries in the home. Instead of throwing money and products at their kids, parents invest time, energy, and wisdom in conversation. Memorable experiences replace superficial entertainment. Saying no doesn't communicate that the parents don't care. It actually convinces the children they are loved. More often than not, those kids mature into healthy adults who can set boundaries for themselves. Life is about more than things and pleasure and stimulation. It's about love and trust.

The Balance We Must Strike

The truth is, leading kids is a balancing act. In fact, all good leadership is a balancing act. It is providing two sides of a coin, both the tough and tender side of it all. We must be both strong and sensitive. Young people need their leaders to be velvet-covered bricks. Velvet on the outside—responsive, accepting, and supportive. Inside, however, we must be bricks—leading by principles, defining boundaries, and holding them to standards. This leadership is both responsive and demanding. It's the best way to prepare kids to become healthy adults. To implement this leadership style, we will likely need to start slow and small. No huge, overnight change. If we are consistent, however, I believe we can lead this positive change.

Let me share with you why this is so vital.

Preventing the Artificial from Replacing the Authentic

In 2012, something unusual happened in Cooperstown, New York. When the envelope was opened to announce the newest inductees into the National Baseball Hall of Fame, no name was inside. No one made the cut. Nada.

This has only happened eight times in professional baseball history. The sad part of this story is, the top candidates were good enough to make it. But voters suspected these players had used performance enhancing drugs to play well—Mark McGuire, Roger Clemmons, Sammy Sosa, Barry Bonds, and the like. A year later it was Ryan Braun, Alex Rodriquez, and dozens of others.

This is a picture of a growing phenomenon in our culture. Slowly, the authentic is being replaced by the artificial: artificial sweeteners, artificial grass, artificial hearts, artificial flowers, artificial Christmas trees, artificial intelligence, even artificial insemination. Those great baseball players? Voters were concerned that they had artificial talent.

It's everywhere. Instead of internal motivation, so many seek external motivation through music or video stimulation. Nothing is wrong with those, but what happens when I have no external source to motivate me? I'm unmotivated. The external stimuli could aptly be called artificial motivation. It's not authentic.

In 2012, I released a book called *Artificial Maturity*. It's about the growing phenomenon of kids who appear to be mature because they know so much but who have actually experienced so little. They have content without context. I believe we've encouraged this by settling for virtual experiences rather than real ones.

I've already suggested my grandparents' generation was quite different from ours. They were working on the farm at 14, working at jobs at 15, leading armies at 17, and getting married at 19. Regardless of whether this was right or wrong, they proved that young people had what it takes pull it off. They were capable.

Today we excuse childish behavior in a 20-year-old, saying, "He's just a kid."

Facebook, video games, texting, YouTube, Hulu…superficial busyness. Music rehearsals, sports workouts, and most homework assignments are good disciplines, but even these are virtual—mere simulators of real life. We're masters of the artificial. We often enable our kids to develop artificial maturity.

Six Ideas to Begin the Journey

If we're going to turn this around, we have to become intentional about our kids' development. I am hopeful we can. Instead of overwhelming our teens with loads of imitations, what if we offered...

- *Meaningful work.* What if we challenged them to get jobs that enabled them to labor, make money, and use their primary gifts?
- *Solitude and reflection.* What if we paid them to read great books and then discussed their meaning and interpreted their value with them?
- *Altruistic projects.* What if we served alongside our kids in charitable projects that benefited people who need our help?
- *Intergenerational environments.* What if we planned gatherings where multiple generations mixed it up in conversation, developing our kids' emotional maturity?
- *Travel.* What if we exposed kids to cultures that are different from ours and talked about the differences and commonalities?
- *Mentors.* What if we introduced kids to our network so they could find mentors in the careers they hope to enter?

Why Not Inoculate Them?

For more than 30 years, I've traveled all over the world. I love travel, especially to remote and exotic places I've never seen in person. Once in a while, I travel to developing nations that require immunizations. Before I'm exposed to certain diseases in other countries, a nurse inoculates me, introducing a small dose of the disease into my body. Over a few weeks, I build up enough antibodies to fight off the disease when I arrive in the foreign country.

In one sense, this is a picture of what we must do for our kids. In order for them to face adversity well, we must introduce small doses of it early on. In order for them to possess the discipline necessary for hard work or stressful jobs, we must expose them to challenges in smaller amounts so they are ready to face larger ones when the time comes. In a sense, they build up antibodies. They become inwardly strong and prepared for what's ahead.

That's the job of a parent. That's what I call preparing the child for the path.

Changing Our Minds About Kids

This chapter is the capstone for the book. It could be the most important chapter for you. I've loaded it with ideas.

Over the last 12 chapters, I've consistently suggested that we need to change our minds about how we raise kids. If we plan on releasing well-adjusted young adults into the world, we must do some adjusting ourselves, focusing on preparing them and not just protecting them.

Recently, I read about Paul Wallich, a father who built a helicopter drone with a video camera to follow his grade-school son to the bus stop. He wants to make sure his son arrives at the bus stop safe and sound. The gizmo undoubtedly provides an awesome show-and-tell contribution. In my mind, however, Paul Wallich gives new meaning to the term *helicopter parent*.

Paul is a picture of so many parents today.

I applaud the engagement of this generation of parents and teachers, but we need to recognize the unintended consequences of our engagement. We want the best for our children, but research now shows that our overprotecting, overconnecting style has damaged them. Let me summarize four categorical errors we've made in raising this generation of kids and how we can rectify our mistakes.

We Risk Too Little

We live in a world that warns us of danger at every turn. Toxic. High Voltage. Flammable. Slippery When Wet. Steep Curve Ahead. Don't Walk. Hazard. This safety-first preoccupation emerged more than 30 years ago with the Tylenol scare and with children's faces appearing on milk cartons. We became fearful for our kids. So we put knee pads, safety belts, and helmets on them—at the dinner table. Okay, I'm kidding, but it's true that we've insulated our kids from risk. Here's how author Gever Tulley put it.

> If you're over 30, you probably walked to school, played on the monkey bars, and learned to high-dive at the public pool. If you're younger, it's unlikely you did any of these things. Yet, has the world become that much more dangerous? Statistically, no. But our society has created pervasive fears about letting kids be independent—and the consequences for our kids are serious.[1]

Unfortunately, overprotecting our young people has had an adverse effect on them.

"Children of risk-averse parents have lower test scores and are slightly less likely to attend college than offspring of parents with more tolerant attitudes toward risk," says a team led by Sarah Brown of the University of Sheffield in the UK. "Aversion to risk may prevent parents from making inherently uncertain investments in their children's human capital; it's also possible that risk attitudes reflect cognitive ability, researchers say."[2] Sadly, this *Scottish Journal of Political Economy* report won't help us unless we do something about it. Adults continue to vote to remove playground equipment from parks so kids won't have accidents, to request that teachers stop using red ink as they grade papers and even refrain from using the word *no* in class. It's all too negative. I understand the intent to protect students, but we are failing miserably at getting them ready for a world that will not be risk free.

Psychologists in Europe are discovering the adverse effects of this overprotection. Interviews reveal that young adults who grew up in risk-free environments are now fearful of normal risks because they never took any risks as kids. The truth is, kids need to fall a few times to learn it's normal; they may even need to skin their knees. Teens likely need to break up with a girlfriend to appreciate the emotional maturity that lasting relationships require.

Taking calculated risks is all a part of growing up. In fact, it plays a huge role. Childhood may be about safety and self-esteem, but as students mature, they need to experience risk and achievement to form their identity and build their confidence. Most kids hunger for it. According to a study by University College in London, risk-taking behavior peaks during adolescence. Teens are apt to take more risks than any other age group. Their brains program them to do so. They must test boundaries and values and find their identity during these years. This is when they must learn through experience the consequences of certain behaviors. Our failure to let them risk may explain why so many young adults between the ages of 22 and 35 still live at home, haven't started their careers, or haven't had a serious relationship. Normal risk taking at 14 or 15 would have prepared them for decisions that require risks.

We Rescue Too Quickly

This generation of young people has not developed some of the life skills kids did 30 years ago because adults swoop in and take care of problems for them. We remove the need for them to navigate hardships.

Staff from four different universities recently told me they encountered students who had never filled out a form or an application. Desiring to care for their kids and not disadvantage them, parents or teachers had always done it for them.

Freshmen in college who receive average grades on projects will immediately call their mothers, right in the middle of class. This happens thousands of times each year. After interrupting the class discussion with a personal complaint about a poor grade, some students actually hand their cell phone to their professor, saying, "My mom wants to talk to you." Yes, Mom attempts to negotiate the grade. Amazing.

In many ways, the role of a parent has changed. The supervisor of 40 years ago has morphed into the Superman of today. At one time, we supervised kids' work as they grew up, but they did the work. Today, we think good parents should rescue children from hardship, not recognizing how this disables those kids later in life. In fact, I believe some parents love the ego fulfillment they receive from playing the superhero.

A Harvard admissions counselor reported that a prospective student looked him in the eye and answered every question he was asked. The counselor felt the boy's mother must have coached him on eye contact because he tended to look down after each response. Later, the counselor learned the boy's mom was texting him the answers every time a question came in.

A college president said a mother of one of his students called him, saying she'd seen that the weather would be cold that day and wondered if he would make sure her son was wearing his sweater as he went to class. She wasn't joking.

Once again, this may sound harsh, but rescuing and overindulging our children is an insidious form of child abuse. It's parenting for the short-term, and it sorely misses the point of leadership—to equip our young people to eventually succeed without our help. Once again, their social, emotional, spiritual, and intellectual muscles can atrophy because they're not exercised.

I learned conflict resolution on a baseball field, where my friends and I had to umpire our own games. I learned discipline by tossing newspapers on driveways at five thirty each morning. I learned patience sitting on a bench as a second-string basketball player. And I cultivated a work ethic closing a fast-food restaurant each night at eleven. Far too often today, parents safeguard kids from many of these experiences.

The fact is, students enjoy being rescued by adults. Who wouldn't? They learn to play parents against each other. They learn to negotiate with faculty for more time, lenient rules, extra credit, and easier grades. This confirms that these kids are not stupid. They learn to play the game. Sooner or later, they know someone will rescue them. If they fail or act out, an adult will smooth things over and remove the consequences for misconduct. I repeat: This isn't even remotely close to how the world works. It actually disables our kids.

We Rave Too Easily

As I mentioned earlier in this book, the self-esteem movement has been around since Baby Boomers were kids, but it took root in our school systems in the 1980s. We determined every kid would feel special regardless of what they did, which meant they began hearing remarks like these:

"You're awesome!"
"You're smart."
"You're gifted."
"You're super!"

We meant well, but research is now indicating this method has unintended consequences. In the chapter called "We Praise the Wrong Things," I discussed the notion that when we affirm our children, we must praise a variable that is in their control. Here I'm suggesting that many of us have simply gone overboard with our praise...period. Anything that plentiful begins to lose its value. When parents notice this, they raise the stakes, exaggerating their comments or talking more loudly as if to convince their kids of their belief in them. Over time, one of two things occur. Either the praise becomes meaningless and the kids stop believing it, or they become addicted to the praise and cannot perform without it.

Neither of these is a good outcome. What's more, kids eventually observe that Mom is the only one who thinks they're awesome. No one else is saying it. They begin to doubt their parents' objectivity. The praise feels good in the moment, but it's not connected to reality.

Dr. C. Robert Cloninger at Washington University in St. Louis has done brain research on the prefrontal cortex, which monitors the reward center of the brain. He says the brain has to learn that frustrating spells can be worked through. The reward center of our brains learns to say, Don't give up. Don't stop trying. "A person who grows up getting too frequent rewards," Cloninger says, "will not have persistence, because they'll quit when the rewards disappear."[3]

When we rave too easily, kids eventually learn to cheat, exaggerate, lie, and avoid the difficulties of real life. They have not been conditioned to face it.

We Reward Too Frequently

Attend a Little League baseball awards ceremony, and you soon learn that everyone's a winner. Everyone gets a trophy. They all get ribbons. This pattern of handling sports, theater, art, dancing, or recitals has overtaken our communities. Have you noticed? I've spoken to moms and dads who've told me...

- Their kids got a ribbon for fifth runner-up.
- Their child got a trophy for best-looking uniform.
- All the kids participating received medals for attendance.

As parents, we give our children ice cream if they're good, chocolate if they're quiet, little gold stars if they eat their greens, and maybe even money if they get good marks at school. It's normal, right? And doesn't research confirm that when lab rats were rewarded for running through a maze, they improved?

Yes, that's true. But we failed to take into account that we don't really care about a rodent's self-esteem, our relationship with it, its sense of autonomy or independence, its interest in trying out bigger mazes of its own accord, and so on *after we stop rewarding it*. Our children are far different from lab rats!

Contrary to popular belief, more studies are emerging demonstrating that when children expect rewards, their performance actually worsens. Yes, you read that right.

> Contrary to popular myth, there are many studies showing that when children expect or anticipate rewards, *they perform more poorly.* One study found that students' performance was undermined when offered money for better marks. A number of American and Israeli studies show that reward systems suppress a student's creativity, and generally impoverish the quality of their work. Rewards can kill creativity, because they discourage risk-taking. When children are hooked on receiving a reward, they tend to avoid challenges, to "play it safe." They prefer to do the minimum required to get that prize...

When an American fast-food company offered food prizes to children for every book they read, reading rates soared. This certainly looked encouraging—at first glance. On closer inspection, however, it was demonstrated that the children were selecting shorter books, and that their comprehension test-scores plummeted. They were reading for junk-food, rather than for the intrinsic enjoyment of reading. Meanwhile, reading outside school (the unrewarded situation) dropped off...Rewards may well increase activity, [but] they smother enthusiasm and kill passion...It would have been smarter to just give the kids more interesting books, as there is plenty of evidence that intrinsically enjoyable activity is the best motivator and performance enhancer.[4]

Studies over many years have found that behavior modification programs are rarely successful at producing lasting changes in attitudes or even behavior. When the rewards stop, people usually return to the way they acted before the program began. More disturbingly, researchers have recently discovered that children whose parents make frequent use of rewards tend to be less generous than their peers...Extrinsic motivators do not alter the emotional or cognitive commitments that underlie behavior.[5]

Real change happens from the inside out, not the outside in. We meant well with each of these errors, but it's time to correct them.

Question: How do you handle risk? Do you tend to resort to rescuing, raving, or offering rewards?

Changing Our Minds About Kids

I believe we need a new strategy—a plan for how we parent, lead, teach, and coach our children. And it must involve parenting for the long term. We need to worry less about today's happiness and more about tomorrow's readiness. Here's a question for you: What if parents, teachers, coaches, youth workers, and employers collaborated to equip kids for life? With that endgame in mind, the results could be amazing.

Sadly, this is rare. Perhaps you've witnessed these scenarios before.

Teachers try so hard to be hip in the classroom, they leave students amused but confused. The faculty members may be in midlife, but they act as if they're Forever 21. Everyone but them sees the incongruity.

Parents try to control their children, filling their schedules with structure, rules, and goals to meet. They hope that if they just push the kids hard enough, those children won't embarrass them or be underachievers.

Coaches try to lecture their way into the hearts of their young players. They often become frustrated that their student athletes have attention spans of about four minutes. It is the classic old-school leader with a new-world team.

These scenarios are far too common. I find adults everywhere who throw their hands in the air in surrender. They don't know how to lead, parent, coach, pastor, or manage today's Generation iY kids. Sometimes adults fail to lead at all. Our world today is so different from the one we grew up in, grown-ups frequently don't make the jump to understand and practice good leadership with their young. So, what are we to do? How should we lead these kids?

We have to change our minds about how to lead our kids. In fact, let me suggest ten shifts we must make in our perspective to lead them well.

1. Don't think *control*, think *connect*.

Too often, our ambition as parents or teachers is to seize control. We want to govern every action and direct each step kids take as they play, work, or study. Studies show that parents who overprogram their young children's schedules often breed rebellious teens. Why? The kids never got to truly be children. Let me remind you: Control is a myth. None of us are actually in control. Effective leaders work to connect with the next generation because once we connect, we build a bridge of relationship that can bear the weight of hard truth. We earn our right to genuinely influence them. The ability to keep kids under control is a by-product of connection.

2. Don't think *inform*, think *interpret*.

As we have seen, this is the first generation of kids that don't need adults to get information. It's coming at them 24 hours a day as they remain connected to their phones and laptops. They have lots of information. What they need from us is interpretation. Their knowledge has no context. They lack wisdom that comes only from years of experience. Adults must help them make sense of all they know. We must help them interpret experiences, relationships, politics, work, and faith through a wise, balanced lens. Discuss together what's behind movie plots, books, and technology. Teach them how to think. Our goal must be to provide them with a healthy worldview.

3. Don't think *entertain*, think *equip*.

I've seen parents who become absolutely consumed with entertaining their children. A website in my community furnishes moms with places to go to keep their kids entertained and happy. I know teachers who approach their classrooms the same way. Desperate to be popular with students, they do anything to keep kids entertained. Here's a better perspective: How can we equip our young people for the future? If we give them relevant tools to succeed and get ahead, they'll stay engaged. Happiness is a by-product. We must quit busying them so they're happy and start enriching them so they're fulfilled. True satisfaction comes from growth.

4. Don't think *do it for them*, think *help them do it*.

Adults have been committed to giving kids a strong self-esteem for 30 years now. We wrongly assumed we could do that by simply telling them they're special and awesome. According to the American Psychological Association, healthy and robust self-esteem actually comes from achievement, not merely affirmation. In our attempt to provide everything they want, we've actually created a new category of at-risk children: middle-class and affluent kids who are depressed because they've never really accomplished anything. We must teach and parent for the long term, not the short term. Sure, doing it yourself is quicker, but transferring a skill is much better.

5. Don't think *impose*, think *expose*.

Kids have been given options since they were preschoolers. They've been able to choose what food to eat, what game to play, where to go on vacation, what sport to play...you name it. So when adults are afraid their kids are falling behind, we tend to impose a rule or a behavior on them. Mandatory conduct is part of life, but it carries negative baggage with it. When students feel forced to do it, they usually don't take ownership of it. It's your idea, not theirs. Outcomes are almost always diminished. Why not think *expose* instead of *impose*? Show them something new. Give them an opportunity they can't pass up. Make it enticing, as if they're going to miss out on something huge if they pass on it. It then becomes their idea. It feels like motivation, not manipulation. I recognize kids must meet certain requirements, but when possible, exposing beats imposing every time.

6. Don't think *prescriptive*, think *descriptive*.

Many kids today have had everything mapped out for them by adults. Recitals, practices, video games, playground time, lessons, phone games...the list could go on and on. As I said earlier, even Lego sets now have diagrams of what to build and how to build it. We're removing the need for kids to use their own imagination and creativity. Instead of prescribing what they should do next, try describing. Describe an outcome or goal and let them figure out how to reach it with their own ingenuity. Kids need adults to set meaningful goals, but we do too much when we give them each step to take. This is where they can begin to develop some of their own ambition and creativity.

7. Don't think *protect*, think *prepare*.

Child abductions, school shootings, the spread of terrorism... threats like these have made adults paranoid about kids' safety. Schools, churches, and homes take precautions to prevent anything bad from occurring. We use helmets, knee pads, safety belts, background checks, and cell phones to protect kids from evil. Sadly, in our obsession over safety, we've failed to prepare children for adulthood. Most college students never graduate, and of those that do, a large percentage move back home. Instead of fearing for them, it's better to recall your entrance into adulthood and discuss what you learned that helped you succeed. The greatest gift parents can give their children is the ability to get along without them.

8. Don't think tell, think ask.

Many kids grow up with adults telling them what to do every hour of the day. Their lives have been thoroughly scheduled, structured, and programmed by adults. This can disable kids. I've met countless college students who have never shared a bedroom, worked a job, or had much free time to use at their discretion. For many, it's their downfall. They aren't ready for freedom; they don't know how to self-regulate. That's why adults must begin doing more asking than telling as these young people mature. We must lead with questions. Why? They must begin to own the answers instead of borrowing answers from an authority. When most kids are told what to do, they don't have to be responsible for outcomes. It wasn't their decision. When we lead with questions, we force them to think, choose, and be accountable.

9. Don't think cool, think real.

Many parents, teachers, principals, coaches, and youth pastors try hard to be hip and emulate what kids are doing. They think that if they can just be like the kids, the kids will like them. In reality, rarely can an adult (especially someone in midlife) pull this off. The result is more often laughable. No doubt we want to be relevant and current with our style and content, but students do not look to adults to be cool. I don't know any kids who gauge coolness by grown-ups. Cool is good, but kids need adults to be authentic. Be who you are as you connect with them, and learn to laugh at yourself. Be self-aware. Know your quirks and blunders. Genuinely listen. Speak with them in a believable, conversational tone. If kids were honest, they'd tell you that the only thing worse than being uncool is being unreal.

10. Don't think *lecture*, think *lab*.

Without fail, when our young people do wrong, the first thing we want to do is lecture them. It's the quickest way to transmit an idea. However, it isn't the best way to transform a life. As adults, we must begin creating environments and experiences from which we can debrief and process truths. Life lessons are to be found everywhere, so travel to new places, meet with influential people, and engage in service projects. Even movies and various forms of amusement can be sources of discovery and discussion in preparation for their future. Think of this shift in your perspective like a science class. Students not only attend a lecture but also experiment in a lab. The lab experience is where students process most effectively. It's where their head knowledge is transformed into a heart of understanding.

When we lead young people this way, they begin to own their growth. Instead of pushing the string, you're pulling it. President Dwight Eisenhower often used a string to explain how to best lead people. If a string is lying straight on a table, pushing it forward doesn't work very well. Pulling the string is the best way to move it.

A year ago, I asked my son to join me on a trip. In fact, I consistently invited him on several trips. When he asked where I was going, the destination never seemed to strike his fancy, so he declined. I knew those trips would be great experiences, but I didn't want to force things, so he stayed home. When I returned, I specifically shared all the cool things that happened. Then I didn't bring up the subject again, nor did I act as if to say, "I told you so."

Recently, I mentioned I was going on another trip and was taking a few students with me. I didn't invite my son. (I wasn't playing games with him—it was a trip I didn't think he'd enjoy.) He hinted, however, that he may want to go with me on a future trip. I said I was open to that idea. Last month, I mentioned I was travelling to a city I'd invited him to earlier. This time, he spoke up and asked if he could go—he actually wanted to join me.

It was his idea, but I was leading him.

Which Are You—the Owl or the Ostrich?

As I travel and meet thousands of teachers, coaches, parents, and youth workers each year, I find they usually fall into two camps: the owls and the ostriches.

These two birds have become symbols of two different approaches to life. The ostrich has come to represent folly. The Scriptures say that God "did not endow her with wisdom or give her a share of good sense" (Job 39:17). Over the years, people have believed that the ostrich buries its head in the sand when it's afraid or wants to hide. This is actually a myth, but we've come to compare this to a human tendency. Woodrow Wilson compared American foreign policy to the bird: "America cannot be an ostrich with its head in the sand." H.G. Wells wrote, "Every time Europe looks across the Atlantic to see the American eagle, it observes the rear end of an ostrich."

In contrast, the owl symbolizes a completely different approach to life. The owl is most alert at night, when danger lurks. It can rotate its head 360 degrees to see any movement. Because it's always on watch, it has developed acute hearing and keen eyesight, even in the dark… perhaps *especially* in the dark. Owls are known for their distinct calls to other birds and species. Most of all, owls have become symbols of wisdom and nobility.

With that in mind, consider this. Which are you—an owl or an ostrich?

Do you have a tendency to hide from bad news or dangerous trends, not wanting to face reality? Do you bury your head in the sand, wanting to escape the necessary changes we must make to prepare kids for the future? Do you hide behind noise and clutter? Do you get lost in routines, hoping to merely survive each school year?

Or do you do your best work in the dark? Are you alert and observing what's happening all around you in culture and among students today? Do you possess the wisdom to address dangerous patterns in kids, helping them to rise above addictive behavior, risk aversion, self-absorption, and entitlement?

Do you run *to* the roar or *from* the roar?

I've been exposed to leaders in all walks of life, and I've found that we're all ostriches or owls. We choose to play defense or offense when it comes to preparing our kids for the world that awaits them. I'm not a pessimist, but I do believe our culture has done a number on today's generation of kids. We live in dark times in which students finish school unprepared to achieve success in their future.

As cliché as this may sound, we must be owls, standing watch in our culture:

- Stay alert in dark and dangerous times. Keep current on cultural stats.

- Observe patterns and diagnose trends in your kids' behavior.

- Respond wisely as you address negative patterns or shortcomings.

- Signal your colleagues, communicating what needs to be done.

Owls are widely believed to have the best night vision in the animal kingdom. May that be said of us as we lead our kids into adulthood.

Kids Are Products of the World We Created

Let me remind you of something before we close this book. As I travel and speak on school campuses, in athletic departments, in companies, or in churches, I constantly hear adults moan about other people's kids. "Those lazy, entitled, coddled slackers are going to ruin our country."

It may be true.

But if it is, I don't blame the kids. Young people are the products of the world adults have created for them. If kids act irresponsibly, could it be that their parents failed to consistently enforce consequences for their poor decisions? If students act entitled, could it be that their parents or teachers coddled them and didn't push them to grow up? If college graduates move home, unprepared for the real world, who failed to prepare them?

After all, kids aren't the ones who have made the movies, written the books, or programmed the violent computer games that are shaping their culture. Perhaps we should expand our use of the word 'delinquent' to include the adults who have failed to responsibly prepare kids for the real world.

The Ultimate Finish

Our children will grow into productive, healthy adults only if we first model the way. They are products of our making. They are reflections of our lives. We must show them the way, not merely tell them. It has been said, "Children have never been good at listening to their elders, but they have never failed to emulate them."

Instead of making the mistakes I've listed in this book, how about we trade them in for some healthy leadership and long-term love? What do you say we try the following exchanges to these mistakes?

1. *We won't let them fail.* Correction: Permit them to try on their own and even fail, and then help them see the value of failure. Enable them to build resilience.

2. *We project our lives on them.* Correction: Find your identity in something other than your kids so you can find pleasure in them becoming who they are wired to become.

3. *We prioritize being happy.* Correction: Communicate with your kids that happiness is a by-product of using their gifts in service to others. Help them find where they can serve best.

4. *We are inconsistent.* Correction: Determine the values you want to embody and the equations you want to enforce, and be firm, steady, and clear as you all live by them.

5. *We remove the consequences.* Correction: As your kids make decisions, allow them to experience the outcomes of those choices—either good or bad. Talk them through and learn from them.

6. *We lie about their potential and don't explore their true*

potential. Correction: Rather than spouting random compliments, help your kids identify their strengths, and then reinforce the development of those primary gifts.

7. *We won't let them fight or struggle.* Correction: Don't step in and rescue your kids from working through difficult situations. Instead, talk them through, helping them to grow on the way.

8. *We give them what they should earn.* Correction: Provide opportunities for your kids to work, achieve goals, and earn some money so they can learn to delay gratification.

9. *We praise the wrong things.* Correction: Affirm the qualities that are in your kids' control, such as honesty or effort, instead of smarts or beauty.

10. *We value removing all pain.* Correction: Instead of automatically eliminating pain, comfort your kids (physically and emotionally), but help them see how pain can improve them.

11. *We do it for them.* Correction: When opportunities arise for your kids to work or correct a problem, be a guide and not a god. Let them have the privilege of doing it themselves.

12. *We prepare the path for the child instead of the child for the path.* Correction: Make decisions with a long-term perspective. You are preparing future adults who must be autonomous most of their lives.

The Proving Ground

Several years ago, my wife and I dropped our daughter, Bethany, off at college. I put on my game face, but it was the hardest thing I'd ever done as a father. I knew this freshman launch at the university was coming. I work with university students and have watched parents drop their kids off at college for decades. What's more, Bethany took a gap year the 12 months before, giving us time to mentally prepare for the big drop-off. Still, that day comes as surprising as a thief, taking your baby from you.

Columnist Michael Gerson reminds us that our ancestors actually thought this parting should take place earlier. Many societies once practiced "extrusion," in which adolescents were sent away to live with friends or relatives right after puberty. This was supposed to minimize the nasty conflicts that come from housing teenagers and their parents in close proximity. Some nonhuman primates have a similar practice, forcibly expelling adolescents from the family group.[6]

But in our country, kids are a prized possession. When we drop them off at college, we're acutely aware of something they are not. I've watched this transition for years. They experience the adjustments that come with a new beginning, and we begin the hard part of letting go. Put another way, they have a wonderful future in which our part naturally fades. So even though I did all I knew to do to prepare Bethany for adulthood, I had to fight back the tears. My wife didn't even try.

Gerson suggests that parenthood offers many lessons in patience and sacrifice. But ultimately, it is a lesson in humility. "The whole parenting journey is a short stage in someone else's story." Until now, we've played a starring role in their story. Now, we are supporting actors at best. And it is sufficient. The most important lesson parents can teach their children is how to flourish without them.

The end of childhood, of course, can be the start of adult relationships between parents and children that are rewarding in their own way. While I'm still their dad, I am now befriending my grown children.

I just got a call from my daughter. She's in the third year of her career and is living far away from home—more than 22 hours of driving away. After spending her first two months with her twentysomething colleagues, she called me.

"Hello?" I said.

"Hey, Dad. How's it going?"

"Oh, hey, Bethany. It's good to hear your voice, baby doll. What's up with you?"

"Oh, not much. I guess I just called to say thanks."

"Wow. That's always nice to hear…but thanks for what?"

"Everything," she quipped.

"Everything?" I was prodding, not sure what was on her mind.

She paused for a minute. "Well, I'm not sure how to say this, but… thanks for getting me ready for life. So many of my friends are so emotionally fragile. They can't seem to handle hard days at work. I don't think many of them are really ready for a full-time job. It got me to thinking—my mom and dad got me ready for these days. And I just wanted to say thank you, Dad."

I got teary again.

That phone call made my day. Actually, it may have made my life.

This is the reward of a parent.

Notes

"I Get an A, You Get a D"

1. "Kids Want More Guidance on Money Matters, yet Parents Lacking as Financial Role Models, T. Row Price Survey Finds," Money Confident Kids, March 2012, media.moneyconfidentkids.com/news/2012-parents-kids-money-survey-release/.

2. Ellen Galinsky, *Ask the Children: What America's Children Really Think About Working Parents* (New York: William Morrow, 1999).

3. Leonard Sax, "What's Happening to Boys?" *Washington Post*, March 31, 2006, www.washingtonpost.com/wp-dyn/content/article/2006/03/30/AR2006033001341.html.

4. Gerry Willis, "College Graduates Move Back Home," CNN Money, 2009, money.cnn.com/2009/07/23/pf/saving/graduates_move_back_home/.

5. Condoleeza Rice and Joel Klein, "U.S. Education Reform and National Security," Council on Foreign Relations, March 2012, www.cfr.org/united-states/us-education-reform-national-security/p27618.

Mistake 1: We Won't Let Them Fail

1. "Teachers Say No-One Should Fail," *BBC News*, July 20, 2005, news.bbc.co.uk/2/hi/uk_news/education/4697461.stm.

2. Michael Ungar, "Nurturing Resilience: The Risk-Takers Advantage," *Psychology Today*, August 21, 2009, www.psychologytoday.com/blog/nurturing-resilience/200908/the-risk-takers-advantage.

3. John Tierney, "Can a Playground Be Too Safe?" *New York Times*, July 18, 2011, www.nytimes.com/2011/07/19/science/19tierney.html?_r=0.

4. John Maxwell, *Failing Forward* (Nashville: Thomas Nelson, 2000), 113-14.

5. Personal interview, March 8, 2012.

6. Ungar, "Nurturing Resilience."

Mistake 2: We Project Our Lives on Them

1. Mark Lepper, David Greene, and Robert Nisbett, "Undermining Children's Intrinsic Interest with Extrinsic Rewards: A Test of the Over-Justification Hypothesis," *Journal of Personality and Social Psychology* 28, no. 1 (1973): 129.

2. Daniel H. Pink, *Drive: The Surprising Truth About What Motivates Us* (New York: Riverhead Books, 2009), 15-33.

3. Madeline Levine, *The Price of Privilege* (New York: Harper Collins, 2006), 17-21.

4. Sam Hananel, "Growing Push to Halt Workplace Bullying," *Associated Press*, March 1, 2013, bigstory.ap.org/article/growing-push-halt-workplace-bullying.

5. Barbara Fiese et al., "Family Stories in the Early Stages of Parenthood," *Journal of Marriage and the Family* 57 (1995), 763-70.

6. J. Bruner, "Life as a Narrative," *Social Research* 54 (1987), 11-32; Daniel McAdams, "The Psychology of Life Stories," *Review of General Psychology* 5 (2001), 100-122.

7. Kate McLean et al., "Selves Creating Stories Creating Selves: A Process Model Of Self-Development," *Personality and Social Psychology Review* 11 (2007), 262-78.

8. Robyn Fivush et al., "Do You Know...The Power of Family History in Adolescent Identity and Well-Being," *Journal of Family Life*, February 23, 2010, www.journaloffamilylife.org/doyouknow.html.

9. Tim Elmore, Habitudes: Images That Form Leadership Habits and Attitudes (Atlanta: Growing Leaders), www.GrowingLeaders.com.

Mistake 3: We Prioritize Being Happy

1. Marilyn Elias, "Psychologists Now Know What Makes People Happy," *USA Today*, December 8, 2002.

2. Elizabeth Kolbert, "Spoiled Rotten," *New Yorker*, July 2, 2012, www.newyorker.com/arts/critics/books/2012/07/02/120702crbo_books_kolbert.

3. Eric Wargo, "Aiming at Happiness and Shooting Ourselves in the Foot," *Observer*, August 2007, www.psychologicalscience.org/index.php/video/aiming-at-happiness-and-shooting-ourselves-in-the-foot.html.

4. *BBC News*, "Genes Play Key Happiness Role," March 5, 2008, news.bbc.co.uk/2/hi/health/7278853.stm.

5. Arthur Levine and Diane Dean, *Generation on a Tightrope* (San Francisco: Jossey-Bass, 2012), np.

6. Kolbert, "Spoiled Rotten."

7. "Massachusetts Principal Calls off Honors Night Because It Could Be 'Devastating' to Students Who Missed the Mark," *FoxNews.com*, March 20, 2013, www.foxnews.com/us/2013/03/20/massachusetts-principal-calls-off-honors-night-because-it-could-be-devastating/.

8. Adapted from Justin Rice, "After Sitting Out with Poor Grades, Latin Academy Swimmer Is Scholar-Athlete of the Month," BBS Sports Blog, February 5, 2013, www.boston.com/schools/extras/bps_sports/2013/02/after_sitting_out_last_years_city_swimming_championships_due_to_poor_grades_cristian_mojica_is_the_b.html.

Mistake 4: We Are Inconsistent

1. Jesse Jayne Rutherford and Kathleen Nickerson, "How Kids and Teens Respond to Consistency," Netplaces, www.netplaces.com/defiant-children/consistency/how-kids-and-teens-respond-to-consistency.htm.

2. Ibid.

3. Graeme Patin, "Busy Parents 'Failing to Teach Children Right from Wrong,'" *Telegraph*, April 29, 2013, www.telegraph.co.uk/education/educationnews/10023731/Busy-parents-failing-to-teach-children-right-from-wrong.html.

4. Bruce Feiler, "Family, Inc." *Wall Street Journal*, February 10, 2013, online.wsj.com/news/articles/SB10001424127887323452204578288192043905634.

5. Ibid.

Mistake 5: We Remove the Consequences

1. Hara Estroff-Marano, *A Nation of Wimps* (New York: Crown Archetype, 2008), np.

Mistake 6: We Lie About Their Potential and Don't Explore Their True Potential

1. Cited in Alex Williams, "The Literary Cubs," *New York Times*, November 30, 2011, www.nytimes .com/2011/12/01/fashion/new-yorks-literary-cubs.html?pagewanted=all.

2. Edward E. Gordon, "Help Wanted: Creating Tomorrow's Workforce," *Futurist* 34 (July-August 2000), no. 4.

3. Alexis Lai, "Blind Student Learns to Read Braille with Lips," *CNN News*, July 17, 2013, http:// www.cnn.com/2013/07/17/world/asia/hong-kong-blind-student-braille-lips/index.html.

4. "Tsang Tsz-Kwan, Blind Student with Limited Finger Sensitivity, Reads Braille with Her Lips, and Kicks Academic Butt," *The Huffington Post*, July 18, 2013, www.huffingtonpost.com/2013/07/18/ tsan-tsz-kwan-blind-student-reads-braille-with-lips_n_3619430.html.

Mistake 7: We Won't Let Them Struggle or Fight

1. Tara Palmeri, "Rich Manhattan Moms Hire Handicapped Tour Guides so Kids Can Cut Lines at Disney World," *New York Post*, May 14, 2013, nypost.com/2013/05/14/ rich-manhattan-moms-hire-handicapped-tour-guides-so-kids-can-cut-lines-at-disney-world/.

2. Tara Palmeri, "Rich Parents Hire Play-Date Consultants to Help Kids Play Better for Private-School Admissions," *New York Post*, July 19, 2013, nypost.com/2013/07/19/ rich-parents-hire-play-date-consultants-to-help-kids-play-better-for-private-school-admissions/.

3. "Top C-level Staff Unload Hasbro Shares—Should Fans Worry?" *My Last Dart*, August 29, 2013, www.mylastdart.com/2013/08/top-c-level-staff-unload-hasbro-shares.html.

4. Cited in Anna Hodgekiss, "Children with Controlling 'Helicopter Parents' Are More Likely to Be Depressed," February 14, 2013, http://www.dailymail.co.uk/health/article-2278596/Chil-dren-controlling-helicopter-parents-likely-depressed.html.

5. Debbie Pincus, "Learned Helplessness," EmpoweringParents, www.empoweringparents.com/ Learned-Helplessness-Are-You-Doing-Too-Much-for-Your-Child.php#.

6. Arthur Levine and Diane Dean, *Generation on a Tightrope* (San Francisco: Jossey-Bass, 2012), 44.

7. Po Bronson and Ashley Merryman, *NurtureShock* (New York: Hachette Book Group, 2009), np.

8. C.W. Washburn, "Adjusting the Program to the Child," *Educational Leadership* (December 1953): 138-47, www.ascd.org/ASCD/pdf/journals/ed_lead/el_195312_washburne.pdf.

9. Bryan Goodwin, "Changing the Odds for Student Success: What Matters Most," Mid-continent Research for Education and Learning, 2010.

10. Cited in Rick Nauert, "Anxiety Disorders More Common in Kids Who avoid Scary Situations," PsychCentral, March 13, 2013, psychcentral.com/news/2013/03/13/anxiety-disorders-more -common-in-kids-who-avoid-scary-situations/52558.html.

11. Suzanne Lucas, "Why My Child Will Be Your Child's Boss," *Money Watch*, June 18, 2012, www .cbsnews.com/8301-505125_162-57455011/why-my-child-will-be-your-childs-boss/.

Mistake 8: We Give Them What They Should Earn

1. "Aubrey Ireland, College Student, Wins Restraining Order Against Helicopter Parents,"

Huffington Post, December 27, 2012, www.huffingtonpost.com/2012/12/27/aubrey-ireland -restraining-order-parents_n_2372043.html.

2. Ibid.

3. Dan Tynan, "Why I'm Cyberstalking My Son," Mashable, December 28, 2012, mashable .com/2012/12/28/cyberstalking-parents/.

4. Robert Sun, "Emotional Fuel and the Power to Motivate Students," *Huffington Post*, May 7, 2013, www.huffingtonpost.com/robert-sun/emotional-fuel-and-the-po_1_b_3232236.html; citing Kou Murayama et al., "Predicting Long-Term Growth in Students' Mathematics Achievement: The Unique Contributors of Motivation and Cognitive Strategies (2012)," *Child Development* (2012).

5. Greg Toppo et al., "When Test Scores Seem Too Good to Believe," *USA Today*, March 17, 2011, usatoday30.usatoday.com/news/education/2011-03-06-school-testing_N.htm.

6. Cited in Paul Mandelstein, *Being a Great Divorced Father: Real-Life Advice from a Dad Who's Been There* (Berkeley: Nolo, 2012), 56.

7. Cited in Emily Alpert, "Kids Like Being Kids, Study Finds, Perhaps Thanks to Parenting," *Los Angeles Times*, July 21, 2013, articles.latimes.com/2013/jul/21/local/la-me-growing-up-20130722.

8. Melissa Bailey, "Zero out of 44 Students Complete Freshman Year," *New Haven Independent*, June 28, 2013, www.newhavenindependent.org/index.php/archives/entry/hsc_freshmen/.

Mistake 9: We Praise the Wrong Things

1. Deepa Fernandes, "Researchers Say Too Much Praise Harms Kids; Parents Hear: Blah, Blah, Blah, Blah (Poll)," Southern California Public Radio, August 14, 2013, www.scpr.org/blogs/ education/2013/08/14/14455/researchers-say-too-much-praise-harms-kids-parents/.

2. Jenny Anderson, "Too Much Praise Is No Good for Toddlers," *New York Times*, October 27, 2011, parenting.blogs.nytimes.com/2011/10/27/too-much-praise-is-no-good-for-toddlers/?_r=0.

3. Jenn Berman, *The A to Z Guide to Raising Happy and Confident Kids* (Novato, CA: New World Library, 2007) ; cited in Heather Hatfield, "The Right Way to Praise Your Kids," December 2, 2012, *WebMD*, www.webmd.com/parenting/guide/the-right-way-to-praise-your-kids.

4. Cited in Hatfield, "The Right Way to Praise Your Kids."

5. Cited in Julie Christensen, "Negative Effects of Too Much Praise from Parents," *GlobalPost*, everydaylife.globalpost.com/negative-effects-much-praise-parents-2799.html.

6. Tom Loveless, "The 2006 Brown Center Report on American Education: How Well Are American Students Learning?" The Brookings Foundation, October 2006, www.brookings.edu/ research/reports/2006/10/education-loveless.

7. Po Bronson and Ashley Merryman, *NurtureShock* (New York: Hachette Book Group, 2009), 20.

8. Carol S. Dweck, *Mindset: The New Psychology of Success* (New York: Random House Publishing Group, 2006); review adapted from Bronson and Merryman, *NurtureShock*.

9. Marguerite Lamb, "7 Secrets to Raising a Happy Child," *American Baby*, May 2008, www.par ents.com/toddlers-preschoolers/development/fear/raising-happy-children/; Bob Murray, *Raising an Optimistic Child: A Proven Plan for Depression-Proofing Young Children—for Life* (New York: McGraw-Hill, 2005).

10. Matt Gottfried, "Heart of a Champion," March 28, 2013, nctennis.com/node/623.

11. Ibid.

12. Ibid.

Mistake 10: We Value Removing All Pain

1. Edwin C. Bliss, *Doing It Now: A 12-Step Program for Curing Procrastination and Achieving Your Goals* (New York: Scribner, 1983), 100.

2. Sally Koslow,"Hey, Baby Boomer Parents, Back Off!" CNN, July 10, 2012, www.cnn .com/2012/07/10/opinion/koslow-adultescents/.

3. See Leonard Sax, *Boys Adrift* (New York: Basic Books, 2007).

4. Seth Godin, *Stop Stealing Dreams*, sethgodin.typepad.com/files/stop-stealing-dreams6print.pdf.

5. Alice Walton,"Is a Little Stress a Good Thing for the Brain?" *Forbes*, April 18, 2013, www.forbes .com/sites/alicegwalton/2013/04/18/is-a-little-stress-a-good-thing-for-the-brain/; citing Eliza-beth D. Kirby et al., "Acute Stress Enhances Adult Rat Hippocampal Neurogenesis and Acti-vation of Newborn Neurons via Secreted Astrocytic FGF2," University of California, Berkeley, April 16, 2013, elife.elifesciences.org/content/2/e00362.

6. Rebecca Klein,"Long Island Middle School Bans Balls to Protect from Injuries," *Huffington Post*, October 8, 2013, www.huffingtonpost.com/2013/10/08/long-island-ball-ban_n_4065353.html.

Mistake 11: We Do It for Them

1. Liz Bibb,"No Easter Bunny at Macon's Central City Park This Year," *Telegraph*, April 5, 2012, www.macon.com/2012/04/05/1976537/no-easter-bunny-at-macons-central.html.

2. Amy Hoak,"How Long Is Too Long to Live with Your Parents?" *Market Watch*, August 14, 2013, www.marketwatch.com/story/how-long-is-too-long-to-live-at-home-2013-08-13.

3. Henry Samuel, "French Mother Caught Sitting Teenage Daughter's Exam," *Telegraph*, June 20, 2013, www.telegraph.co.uk/news/worldnews/europe/france/10132957/French-mother-caught -sitting-teenage-daughters-exam.html.

4. Justin Pope, "Study: Parental Support Sends Down College GPA," Associated Press, January 15, 2013, finance.yahoo.com/news/study-parental-support-sends-down-145802985.html.

5. Lenore Skenazy, *Free Range Kids* (Hoboken, NJ: Jossey-Bass, 2010).

6. Deborah Leong and Elena Bodrova, *Tools of the Mind: A Vygotskian Approach to Early Child-hood Education* (Upper Saddle River, NJ: Prentice Hall, 1995); cited in Po Bronson and Ash-ley Merryman, *NurtureShock: New Thinking About Children* (New York, Hachette Book Group, 2009), 155.

7. Bradford Smart, *Topgrading* (New York: Penguin, 2005), np.

Mistake 12: We Prepare the Path for the Child Instead of the Child for the Path

1. "To Ensure Every Child 'Wins', Ontario Athletic Association Removes Ball from Soccer," CBC Radio, September 3, 2013, www.cbc.ca/thisisthat/blog/2013/09/03/to-ensure-every-child-wins -ontario-athletic-association-removes-ball-from-soccer/index.html.

2. Seth Godin, *Stop Stealing Dreams*, sethgodin.typepad.com/files/stop-stealing-dreams6print.pdf.

3. *And Now for Something Completely Different: An Introduction to Sudbury Valley School* (Framing-ham, MA: Sudbury Valley School Press, 1995), 6.

4. Marguerite Lamb, "7 Tips to Raising a Happy Child," *American Baby*, May 2008, www.parents .com/toddlers-preschoolers/development/fear/raising-happy-children/; citing Edward M. Hal-lowell, *The Childhood Roots of Adult Happiness* (New York: Ballantine Books, 2003).

5. Lamb, "7 Secrets to Raising a Happy Child," citing Bonnie Harris, *When Your Kids Push Your Buttons and What You Can Do About It* (New York: Warner Books, 2003).

6. Ibid.

Changing Our Minds About Kids

1. Gever Tulley, *Beware Dangerism* (TED Books, 2011).

2. Sarah Brown et al., "Parental Risk Attitudes and Children's Academic Test Scores: Evidence from the US Panel Study of Income Dynamics," *Scottish Journal of Political Economy* 59, no. 1, February 2012.

3. C. Robert Cloninger, *Feeling Good: The Science of Well-Being* (New York: Oxford University Press, 2004), np.

4. Robin Grille, "Rewards and Praise: The Poisoned Carrot," National Child Project, www.naturalchild.org/robin_grille/rewards_praise.html.

5. Alfie Kohn, "The Risk of Rewards," *ERIC Digest*, December 1994, www.alfiekohn.org/teaching/ror.htm.

6. Michael Gerson, "Saying Goodbye to My Child, the Youngster," Washington Post, Opinions, August 19, 2013, www.washingtonpost.com/opinions/michael-gerson-saying-goodbye-to-my-child-the-youngster/2013/08/19/6337802e-08dd-11e3-8974-f97ab3b3c677_story.html.

Acknowledgments

Like all worthwhile projects, this book is the product is many hands and many minds. I'd like to thank Holly Moore and our Growing Leaders team for their consistent support as this book took shape. Each of them was involved in digging up research and finding statistics and stories so I could share them in a logical manner. I am grateful to Andrea Pompili for carving out days for me to write. Many thanks to Dr. Greg Doss, who dug up primary research and was stellar in the process. Thank you Caleb Perkins, Ashley Priess, and Chelsea Vilchis for researching and footnoting. Thanks Anne Alexander for proofing the manuscript and providing edits and ideas to make the book stronger. Thanks Chris Harris for communicating to our tribe through social media. Finally, thanks to my family—my wife, Pam, and kids, Bethany and Jonathan—who've served as a laboratory for these ideas all of their lives.

I love you all.

Want Some More Ideas?

Dr. Tim Elmore is president and founder of Growing Leaders, a nonprofit organization that resources schools, companies, universities, athletic teams, organizations, and families to equip students to grow into healthy adults and effective leaders. Growing Leaders offers events, books, videos, podcasts, courses, articles (blogs), and digital content that empower adults to connect with young people and equip them to be ready for adulthood.

Our most popular resource, a series called Habitudes—Images That Form Leadership Habits and Attitudes, has sold hundreds of thousands of copies. Here are other books Tim Elmore has written that parents have found helpful:

Nurturing the Leader Within Your Child

Life-Giving Mentors

Generation iY—Our Last Chance to Save Their Future

Habitudes: Images That Form Leadership Habits and Attitudes (Series)

Soul Provider: Becoming a Confident Spiritual Leader at Home and Work

52 Leadership Ideas You Can Use with Students

Artificial Maturity: Helping Kids Meet the Challenge of Becoming Authentic Adults

Visit our website at www.GrowingLeaders.com.

To learn more about Harvest House books and
to read sample chapters, visit our website:

www.harvesthousepublishers.com

HARVEST HOUSE PUBLISHERS
EUGENE, OREGON